Bereavement,

Loss

and Learning Disabilities

A Guide for Professionals and Carers

Robin Grey

Jessica Kingsley Publishers
London and Philadelphia

All case histories used in this book are fictional but are based on typical presentations of people who have experienced bereavements and losses.

First published in 2010
by Jessica Kingsley Publishers
116 Pentonville Road
London N1 9JB, UK
and
400 Market Street, Suite 400
Philadelphia, PA 19106, USA

www.jkp.com

Library of Congress Cataloging in Publication Data
Grey, Robin, 1962-
  Bereavement, loss and learning disabilities : a guide for professionals and carers / Robin Grey.
       p. cm.
  Includes index.
  ISBN 978-1-84905-020-3 (alk. paper)
  1. Bereavement. 2. People with mental disabilities--Psychology. 3. People with mental disabilities--Means of communication. I. Title.

BF575.G7G698 2010
155.9'37087--dc22

                                   2009032406

British Library Cataloguing in Publication Data
A CIP catalogue record for this book is available from the British Library

ISBN 9781849050203

Printed and bound in Great Britain by
MPG Books Limited

CONTENTS

This book is dedicated to the memory of
Dr Christine Cooper
(1918–1986)
without whom my life would have been different

1

Introduction and Overview

The purpose of this book

Since the mid-1980s there has been a significant change in the way that society views people with learning disabilities. Services have adapted well on the whole and the quality of life for many people has changed considerably. Care is provided in a much more person-centred way, with people being able to influence the way that they make choices and having a much greater control over their lives. The advent of person-centred planning is evidence of this.

There has also been a major change in the way that society talks about bereavement. Although bereavement is still a private affair for families and individuals, it is now easier for people who experience grief to talk about it with others. Bereavement counselling is more widely available and is seen as being a helpful way of coping with grief. We are also encouraged to talk about our feelings when facing distress or when we find it difficult to cope with stress, anger and depression.

Despite this change in society, many people still find it hard to talk about their experience of bereavement and other losses that can have a significant impact (on people with learning disabilities), such as loss of status and equality, loss of health, loss of relationships, loss of employment and loss of independence. Bereavement is a normal life event that has to be managed, however difficult. Having a learning disability can complicate this further. For someone on the autistic spectrum, for example, linking a loss to an identified feeling and then putting it into words can be too difficult when there is a struggle to process events and emotions.

There is also a reluctance to talk about learning disabilities as an issue if it is not in people's immediate experience. Disability issues in general are still partly invisible, although there is greater awareness of access and health in general than in the past. There has been a significant shift in providing learning disabilities services in mainstream settings.

The history of learning disability over the past hundred years has recently come into focus and there has been some interest in archiving learning disabilities in terms of social history (the British Institute of Learning Disabilities has a list of publications on this subject at www.bild.org.uk). Part of this history includes how people with learning disabilities were excluded from the everyday experiences of loss and grief. Freud (1904) stated that 'a certain measure of natural intelligence and ethical requirement' was necessary in order for talking therapy to be considered. People with disabilities were thought to lack these requirements and so they were overlooked for many years.

In the past people with learning disabilities tended not to be told about the death of family or friends. Perhaps this was because their needs as adults were not recognized or there was an assumption that they would be unable to understand or they needed to be 'protected from grief'. Protecting 'the disabled' from news of grief was common, despite the reality that they were surrounded by it.

In fact people with learning disabilities grieve just as much as anyone else. How support is given to them will vary according to each individual. Sometimes direct help beyond practical changes is not required, but an understanding of how to help is essential.

People with learning disabilities are assuming a greater importance as a client group. Advocates of social policy are having to recognize their specific health needs. The growth of individualized care services reflects a real change in how we approach clients' physical and psychological health. An understanding of the impact of losses and the way that these translate into clients' everyday lives is important if we are able to help people to move forward from their experience.

Advances in health care mean that having a learning disability need not equate to having a shorter life expectancy. There are opportunities for greater independence as the provision of services has widened. However, people with a learning disability are now more likely to be exposed to loss and bereavement. The assumption that clients will die before their parents, common in the past, will not always be true.

Since the late 1990s in particular there has been a bigger picture of change around social policy. The rights and needs of people with disabilities in general and learning disabilities in particular have been represented on a much broader platform. While there had been improvements in integration, the rights of individuals needed to be pushed up the political and social agenda. This is still in process but has afforded much greater protection and visibility to people with learning disabilities. Anyone who works with or cares for people with learning disabilities is now more acutely aware of how having such a disability can have a direct impact on an individual's mental health and can make someone more vulnerable to developing a significant mental health problem. The reasons for this are complex but a history of loss where community medical and psychological help have not been available in the right way will have contributed to a person's distress.

For some clients, a loss can be the start of a change that leads to having a more independent life but is a struggle as it is worked through. The psychological impact can be unpredictable. For professionals working in this area, it can be difficult to access our own thoughts and feelings. We can be left to carry some of the grief and loss of an individual or family. The unconscious processes that are involved not only can be powerful but also may offer a route into understanding.

This book aims to give some context to how people with learning disabilities experience loss and bereavement and how the situation can be managed. There have been many changes in policy. Attitudes and services have, on the whole, changed for the better. With this comes a responsibility to provide services that acknowledge that there is a greater exposure to loss and change. This has to be met in a way that values the individual's emotional needs and does so in a way that respects the clients we work for. The book offers some suggestions on how to approach learning disabilities work if you have contact with people who are grieving and have experienced loss.

Terminology

The term 'learning disabilities' is used throughout this book. This term is defined by the World Health Organization (1980) as 'a state of arrested or incomplete development of mind'. Learning disabilities is classified as being applied to those with an intelligence quotient (IQ) of 70 or below, following the work of Alfred Binet, a French psychologist of the early twentieth century. An IQ measurement of 50–70 indicates mild learning disability, 35–50 indicates moderate learning disability, 20–35 indicates severe learning disability and below 20 indicates profound learning disability. IQ measurements are the guide used to assess the degree of learning disability, but they do not take into account other skills that a person may have or the skills that someone uses to indicate social functioning or emotional reasoning.

Our emotional responses to change, and in particular to bereavement and loss, are dictated by a number of factors; although IQ measurement may indicate how someone is likely to process or manage their emotions, their actual reactions will depend on a number of different factors. There are particular considerations about the vocabulary that is used to define and describe death that will be explored later in this book.

The effect of 'labelling' people can be profoundly damaging in many instances. The wider notion of disability can empower and terminology is all part of that. D'Ardenne and Mahtani (1989) state that 'many disabled people prefer the term "disabled people" because it refers to disablement as something that society does to individuals, rather than the personal characteristics of impairment' (D'Ardenne and Mahtani 1989, p.35). This indicates that as a means to describe a process, terms around disabilities can convey use and abuse of power.

Although we use the term 'bereavement' now, the root of this term comes from the Old English term *reafian*, which means to 'deprive' or 'rob'.

Facts and figures

The subject of bereavement and loss has to be set in the context of comparatively recent statistics. The Foundation for People with Learning Disabilities (2007) estimates that 985,000 people in the United Kingdom have a learning disability, which equates to about 2 per cent of the population. Of these 796,000 are over the age of 20. In 2004 it was estimated, however, that only 20 per cent of this population were known to learning disabilities services. The same foundation found that 60 per cent of the people known to services lived with their families. It estimates that by 2021 there will be over 1 million people with learning disabilities over the age of 15 and the number of adults with learning disabilities over the age of 60 is predicted to rise by 36 per cent between 2001 and 2021.

Similar percentages for populations are quoted by associations for people with learning disabilities in the United States, Canada and Australia.

Relevant UK legislation and policy

Since the 1990s there has been some positive legislation in the UK that has improved the lives of people with learning disabilities and the way that they can gain support to live more independent lives. This has afforded people greater protection at times of risk and change and also greater rights in terms of how they live their lives. The National Health Service (NHS), education and social services have all improved so that on the whole, the agenda for rights and choices has been pushed forward.

Advocacy services have taken a responsibility for enabling people with learning disabilities to take a greater role in their own lives. At times of change and transition such services can be valuable mediators for what people want themselves. The relevant legislation in the UK is outlined below. Please see Useful Organizations and Resources for international legislation.

Valuing People White Paper 2001

In the UK, the *Valuing People* White Paper (Department of Health 2001b) has been an important change in the way that people with learning disabilities are able to access health services and has, on the whole, improved the culture of seeking help when necessary as well as setting an expectation that the right care will be provided.

Although bereavement and loss are primarily psychologically based issues, the issue of access to wider care has been crucial in enabling greater joined-up thinking in the way that care is provided to individuals. Reducing health inequalities was one of the main aims of *Valuing People*. This built on the principles set out in John O'Brien's Five Accomplishments (1989), which provided a framework for services for people with learning disabilities and outlined how their lives could be improved through clear thinking around rights and responsibilities and a change in policy thinking.

Mental Capacity Act 2005

In the UK, the Mental Capacity Act 2005 (subsequently 2007 in Scotland) stated that there may be times when individuals (not only those with learning disabilities) are not deemed capable of making decisions on their own behalf (Department of Health 2007a). In such situations decisions may need to be taken in the best interests of those concerned. This is particularly relevant if following a bereavement or major change, it is felt necessary to assess someone's capacity to make decisions that will ultimately ensure their future and safety. The Mental Health Act 2007 also addressed how people who were under extreme stress or vulnerability could be safely cared for should they need it under specific terms and conditions (Department of Health 2007b).

National Service Frameworks

National Service Frameworks were introduced in the UK in order to ensure national health care standards. This means that everyone should receive the same level of care outlined for specific conditions. Learning disabilities is included in this under the category for long-term conditions.

Partnership working is an important part of the ethos and practice for the National Service Frameworks. This has meant that services should be more accessible and communication should be strong between the different agencies involved in people's care. In terms of the way that this works for people with learning disabilities, it means that when faced with any kind of transition, for example a bereavement which necessitates change, all the services should work together for the benefit of the client. The National Service Frameworks have made significant progress in enabling people with learning disabilities to have real choice about how they live their lives.

Context of the work

Society is much more 'grief aware' nowadays but there is still fear and denial around it at times. People can exaggerate fears particularly when they are about health where outcomes are uncertain. Some physical health conditions are more common in learning disabilities such as epilepsy (associated with neurology) and dementia (especially in older clients with Down syndrome). These conditions can be managed but have an increased risk attached to longer-term outcomes.

Other conditions, such as Asperger syndrome and autism, can be more complex in terms of understanding the impact of bereavement and change.

People with learning disabilities have an increasing number of options in terms of the services that they access and how their care is delivered. In the UK the direct payments scheme is an arrangement for people who want to receive council payments themselves so that they can pay for and manage their own support and care. However, individuals have to give consent for this and have the ability to manage their own buying of services even if they need support to do so. The scheme has enabled a number of people to feel that they have greater choice and control over their own lives.

However, there are occasional cases where the needs of clients are not adequately met when facing medical emergencies, either by the lack of communication between services or from eligibility criteria being questioned leading people to be passed from one range of services to another.

Sudden death is not uncommon. People with learning disabilities are more prone to degenerative and neurological conditions. They are also more likely to witness or experience more illness and drama related to health concerns and crises. Ambulances and paramedics can be regular visitors at day centres where people have epilepsy for example.

Perhaps the greatest source for help for those who are grieving can be found within the learning disabilities community itself. Many people with learning disabilities, particularly those of similar ages, will have shared common experiences and so may more easily understand what others are experiencing. Organizations such as the British Institute of Learning Disabilities (BILD) and People First have been instrumental in setting up and facilitating such groups. For details of these and international organizations, please see Useful Organizations and Resources.

The focus of different practitioners

The help, support and care provided to an individual following bereavement will often lead to a range of referrals to different professionals, including psychologists, community nurses and occupational therapists. In learning disabilities work, speech and language therapists can help to facilitate communication. Audiologists together with hearing therapists can often help if someone has a congenital or age-related hearing loss condition. Behavioural practitioners can help people who find it hard to grasp the reality of loss and can make suggestions for managing change.

Social workers (now known as care managers in the UK) have a key role in liaising with families and agencies about future care needs. There may also be a related mental health team that can address any mental health distress following bereavement and change. Counsellors and psychotherapists have a key role in offering clients a safe space to talk through the impact of what has happened.

Residential and day care staff are probably the people who have the most contact with bereaved clients on a daily basis. Their role is crucial in providing a sense of continuity to people when there may be a sense of internal chaos following the change that has happened.

One care manager commented about one woman who had autism that:

> going to the day centre was the one place that kept her going…she had friends and familiar people there and during that first month she knew that she could rely on the routine of the centre. It made her feel safe when everything else had been chaotic. (Personal communication)

Routine as safety

Having a predictable routine can be very reassuring, particularly when your everyday life has been turned upside down. Anyone who has experienced job loss, moving home or a personal bereavement can identify with this. The need to keep a sense of routine can be very important to many people with learning disabilities and a prolonged alteration to this or a time of not knowing what the future has in store in terms of where you will live or who will support you can create extra unnecessary stress.

In his book *Adult Day Services and Social Inclusion: Better Days*, Chris Clark (2001) identifies five areas of need that can be provided by day services. First, he points to the need for provision of physical care and shelter that can help to protect against the deterioration of physical and mental health; second, the importance of social interaction with others; third, the teaching and development of new social skills and life skills to prepare for greater independence; fourth, to give the opportunity for positive achievements and learning and fifth, the importance of social integration, preparing for employment and independent living.

The acquisition of skills is very important as protective factors following change or bereavement. It is evident that people with learning disabilities who are having to move or who are adapting to a new environment or living at home on their own after living with an elderly relative or carer are better able to cope if they have a flexible and safe routine that can adapt to change. It can be traumatic and disruptive to have to acquire new skills at the same time as grieving; preparing for the future by thinking ahead can ease this process considerably.

Is talking therapy the appropriate treatment?

Following a period of change such as a major life event or bereavement, it is sometimes recommended that clients have some talking therapy to discuss the impact of what has happened with an independent professional. Depending on the individual client, talking therapy can facilitate change and lead to some resolution. Talking therapy has become a popular treatment of choice for anyone who may be experiencing loss, anxiety or depression and it has become more widely used in supporting people with learning disabilities.

With all referrals for learning disabled clients who are grieving, it can take time to assess what the impact of bereavement is and to come up with a plan about how to engage professionals to help. In terms of psychological intervention there are a number of different models and choices that may be available, including systemic or family therapy, psychodynamic therapy and cognitive behavioural therapy. This will often be dependent on what the recommended treatment is.

Problems that may be faced

The impact of losing someone can be devastating for many of us regardless of our existing social networks and the inner resources that we can draw upon. The reasons why bereavement can be more difficult for people with learning disabilities are outlined in the next chapter but they can be summarized as being within the following areas: cognitive, emotional, social, and power and authority.

Cognitive

It can be hard to intellectualize or make sense of bereavement for someone with a learning disability. Grief can become confusing especially when the events surrounding it appear to be out of context. When changes happen without a reason that can be easily explained, then grief is likely to be harder as it is difficult to build a perspective on how and why it happened.

Some people with learning disabilities see things in quite concrete terms but finding a reason for a loss can be hard especially if there is no logic preceding it. If someone's routine is altered on account of the bereavement, this too can be hard to get used to.

Emotional

Individual emotional responses to the loss of someone can vary from person to person. Being able to identify and experience emotions in line with an expected grief reaction is a good indicator of so-called 'healthy' grieving. It is common for people with learning disabilities to be able to experience the emotion but not name the emotion concerned. Emotions can sometimes initially appear to be dependent on how other people think that one *should* react and it is only later that the latent emotions present themselves.

Social

The scope of social relationships that someone with learning disabilities may have will vary considerably. Some people have a large network of friends and neighbours who may have known their family for many years or there can be a number of friendships built up through school and college or day centre contacts that people will have known for a long time. Many people will not have had these experiences, however, and their disability may have meant that they kept themselves to themselves. Following bereavement there can be a smaller network to draw upon and meeting new people following loss can be difficult for them.

Power and authority

Coping with bereavement can highlight to some people their lack of confidence. A period of readjustment is needed after any major life change. When this is accompanied by an existing difficulty in conceptual understanding, it can leave someone with a learning disability feeling as if their self-esteem has been affected. This in turn often has an impact on power and authority issues such as speaking up for yourself and being assertive.

As people with learning disabilities are already dependent on others for a number of practical and emotional aspects of their lives, the impact of experiencing bereavement can be significant. The loss of power that many people feel in having a learning disability is magnified at times of grief.

Associated losses

A consequence of bereavement and major change can be the associated losses that follow it. For example, when individuals experience the loss of a parent or main carer while they are living with them, this is likely to be accompanied by subsequent changes such as moving, changing routines and ending some activities.

Facing this can be hard for people who have not had major change in their lives or for whom change has been associated with trauma or previous grief. Some of the associated losses experienced are briefly outlined below.

Loss of identity

Any major life event can be accompanied by a change in the way that people see themselves in relation to others. People with learning disabilities often experience the loss of someone else as being a more profound loss because of what that figure represented to them. The dependency on family members and paid carers to facilitate social interaction and opportunity to meet others, for example, means that when the carer dies, leaves or moves on, there is less motivation to reinforce or maintain that social interaction, leading to greater risk of identity being lost.

Exclusion from mourning

Some people with learning disabilities find it difficult to take an active role in the necessary actions that follow bereavement. It can feel overwhelming and difficult to know how and where to begin, following the death of someone. However, there are some tasks in which they may be able to take part. Being consulted and asked what they would like is valuing both their role and the relationship that has been lost. The exclusion that can sometimes happen can add to the difficulties following bereavement; encouraging people to take an active role is important.

Loss of independence

Another associated loss can be the loss of independence especially when another person has facilitated that. Moving can be associated with opportunities but in the short to medium term can lead to a loss of independence as a new set of skills and a new environment have to become familiar. Disruption following loss and change can have profound consequences for many of us and a time of readjustment can be painful and demanding. Change of this sort can result in a real move forward in terms of skills learned. This is more so for adults with learning disabilities and coping with change can be a challenge.

Loss of sexuality

Bereavement does not just concern the loss of parents. Until greater awareness of sexuality needs since the 1990s, having a learning disability has meant a denial or lack of recognition of sexual needs. It is not uncommon for people to experience the death of partners, thus affecting their subsequent relationship and sexual needs.

Loss of opportunity

As well as presenting new opportunities in the longer term, a loss or change can take with it routines and further opportunities to develop what is already within the familiar environment that someone lives in. Plans can be disrupted and have to be altered, the chance to develop new skills leading on from existing learning can be brought to an abrupt halt. An individual may have imagined their future always being in the same town, but following the death of their parents may have had to move to a different part of the country.

Loss of culture

Following a loss or major change there can be a disconnection with a person's past and history, which can be the source of much grief and mourning. There is a task involved in this of keeping a continuation or link with the past and this can be found through someone's culture and the continuation of rituals and anniversaries that are celebrated by others. When facing change through circumstances arising from loss, it is important to try to retain as much of the individual's past culture as possible as this is an integral part of someone's identity.

Helplessness

It is common for people who experience loss and bereavement to feel helpless in the face of what has happened. For people with learning disabilities this can be compounded: having a disability can make people feel powerless yet one can achieve a greater sense of empowerment through the help and support that others can give. A major loss or bereavement can bring that familiar helplessness back. Understandably, there is a desire to blame self and others for what has happened but when facing bereavement, in particular, there is very little that can be changed.

A reaction to feeling helpless can be to seek out short-term solutions to the stress that is experienced. These solutions can result in noticeable changes in behaviour, some of which pose a risk to self and others such as behavioural changes, self-harm, alcohol or gambling.

Of course, it is not just bereavement that can trigger reactions of helplessness. People with learning disabilities can build up strong supportive relationships with people who work with them. In a study of this topic, Mattison and Pistrang (2000, p.61) stated that 'residents seemed appreciative and grateful for having an attachment with someone who seemed to be "holding them in mind"'.

Staff in residential services, day care services and other settings become very important and can provide the missing link of friendship, physical and emotional support. Some of these relationships are intimate by their very nature and may indicate a change in the way that someone has begun to trust if they have had negative relationships in the past.

When an individual worker leaves, it can be devastating for the client concerned and they can feel angry and helpless to change the situation. It is this passivity that can contribute to the dependency that many people can experience.

Loss of relationship with someone who shares your experience

Many people with learning disabilities have formed lifelong friendships and relationships where they have shared common experiences sometimes over decades. Geography and location may have meant that they attended the same special school, college and day centre for years. When an individual moves away, forgets, becomes ill or dies, the separation is much more acute. The shared life experience is a defining feature of people's histories and is experienced in the memories that both people share. Losing someone's memory, as happens in some forms of dementia, can be a painful withdrawal of a connection that defined personal experience characterized by loneliness and emotional pain.

Physical sensations

A common response in the early weeks following bereavement is to experience physical sensations as the body reacts to the shock of the news of a death. These can continue depending on the level of stress that is carried by individuals. Tightness in the chest, lack of energy, oversensitivity to noise or physical feeling, breathlessness, feeling faint, are all physical reactions to grief and are likely to be experienced as such.

Communicating physical changes and symptoms can be hard to do if someone feels embarrassed or fearful. It may be that the individual believes that others will be thinking that they are making a fuss or may be carrying fear that there is genuinely something wrong.

Psychic or spirit sensations

Following bereavement or separation it is also common for people to believe that they are being accompanied by the person who has recently died. This can be a belief based on an experienced feeling and can be confusing for someone who may not be used to this. Often these sensations do pass or take on a different sense for the person concerned, but it is important not to minimize them if they are a comfort.

If these sensations persist in a way that is distressing for someone or persist, risking symptoms of hallucinations, then other advice may be needed in order to keep the individual feeling safe.

Collective grief

The death of Princess Diana, Princess of Wales in 1997 was notable in the way that grief can be experienced collectively within a large part of the community. It became a kind of touchstone that people could identify with and that they could project their own loss and sadness on to.

On a smaller but perhaps more intimate scale, people who attend day services or who live in larger residential services or neighbouring developments often experience a kind of collective grief where someone who has been known to that service dies. Sharing the experience and giving and receiving support can enable people to feel more connected in a way that they have not before. Sometimes this can be accessed through shared memories, other times through a shared belief or faith or through interpersonal contact.

One of the positive consequences of sharing or experiencing grief with other people – despite it being about loss and sadness – is that it normalizes the grief reaction. As a number of people are likely to share in the experience it gives individuals something to look back on as they mark the occasion together with others. It is particularly helpful when people with learning disabilities are able to do this as it validates their experience and limits the discomfort that may be anticipated.

Witnessing other people's illness

People with learning disabilities are exposed to a much greater amount of loss through the experience of being with others in a similar position. It is common for a young adult with learning disabilities to be able to name four or five people who they went to school with but who died during the time they were at school. The life expectancy of many people with learning disabilities is less than the general population. Life-threatening and deteriorating health conditions make some people more vulnerable to illness and it is common for others to have been witness to this distress and to speak of it more frequently. Alternatively if people feel unable to speak of their grief, it is more likely to be expressed in behavioural terms.

Day centres are other venues where seizures and other crises are witnessed by others and become part of the drama of daily life. It is common for ambulances to be called and what would have been viewed as shocking in other situations becomes normal and routine. Where someone hears of news of the death of another person that they know and have maybe lived with in a shared house or seen each day at a centre, there can be a question or doubt about whether or not there is anything that they could have done. The concept of 'survivor guilt' can be strong in this area of work (thinking why have I survived when he or she has not).

Conclusion

Loss and bereavement can be experienced as routine life events. It is more likely that people with learning disabilities will experience the death of peers and accelerated losses associated with having fewer options and less control in their life.

Key points from this chapter

- Bereavement and consequent losses can start a whole process of change that can be extremely hard to cope with at a time of mourning. The impact of loss can extend beyond the death of a person.

- People with learning disabilities may have behavioural reactions to grief as well as emotional reactions. There is no one right way of mourning, although delayed grieving seems to be more common.

- Families and staff can become very important figures in supporting people with learning disabilities at times of grieving. It is essential to recognize the breadth of the impact of many bereavements and the compound losses that it can result in.

- It can be hard to witness other people's losses especially when their grief is acute but it is important to be aware of the increased exposure that many people with learning disabilities have to the sudden or expected death of others.

- Bereavements and losses can be major contributory factors towards some individuals becoming unwell in terms of their mental health.

2

How Bereavement and Loss can be Different in Learning Disabilities

Introduction

The process of bereavement and grieving is a complex one, yet one that is understood and socially sanctioned by society even if it is still slightly hidden. For people with learning disabilities, there is a risk that their needs become marginalized and their voice not fully heard. Decisions following bereavement often have to be made at times of great stress and shock, especially if they were living with a sole parent or carer and this can further complicate the situation faced. It is easy to overlook the specific difficulties that may be faced.

Why the experience of bereavement might be different for someone with a learning disability

There are a number of reasons why the grief process may be different for people with learning disabilities. It is also complicated by the many losses that accompany bereavement in terms of change of circumstances which are often specific to this group. Grieving when someone dies or finding change stressful are normal emotional responses, however, and have to be seen as such. Having a learning disability will not automatically mean that someone's experience will be different but there is a greater chance that care will need to taken at such times.

The experiences of people with learning disabilities often come under the heading of 'complicated grief' and there is some truth in this as several factors can affect the grief process. The particular challenges to be faced are discussed in the following sections.

Historical context

Historically, the losses experienced by the learning disabilities population in long-stay hospitals were overlooked or, at best, safely contained. Being in hospital settings meant that there was less exposure to loss as well. Any expression of loss would be likely managed as if it was a behavioural problem, especially if it persisted for too long. In their book *Forgotten Lives: Exploring the History of Learning Disability*, Atkinson, Jackson and Walmsley (1997) write about the importance of recalling the past and with it the sense of loss that was part of people's lives.

Freud concluded that people with learning disabilities could not make use of psychologically based talking therapies. As a whole culture and tradition of psychotherapy and psychoanalysis developed as a way of addressing loss and bereavement among other presenting concerns, it was thought that people with learning disabilities could not be helped in this way.

Since the early twentieth century there has been massive social change and advances in our insight into psychological approaches. Particularly since the 1980s changes in social policy have transformed the lives of people with learning disabilities in general. Although there is still a sense that as a community there is a way to go, the availability of services and the rights of individuals have been progressing and have being integrated into social and health policy. The psychosocial context in which people live their lives has enabled this change to happen.

Emotional changes following bereavement

The changes brought about by bereavement can be sudden and unexpected, especially if there has been no warning that the deceased person was ill. Having a learning disability can minimize the chance to conceptualize the idea that death will happen to others at some point.

When a death and resulting change happens – particularly if the individual has lived with an elderly parent and not much thinking had been done to prepare for the future – there is likely to be an adjustment that can feel too quick too soon. An unfamiliar system can fall into place that can leave the individual feeling confused and disorientated. This can result in emotional and behavioural change for some people as their world feels as if it has been turned upside down.

Decisions have to made urgently, often by other people, resulting in greater safety but less control. Unfamiliar assessments can begin from people who are taking a case on for the short term and who may not have a previous relationship with the individual. Although there is a recognized sensitivity in how these are done, it can be disorientating for individuals who are still struggling to accept the reality of recent change. Getting the pace right can often be a problem for people and is dependent on the help that is seen to be needed.

One mother commented on this when looking back on her experience:

> When my husband died, it was chaos – lots of people in the house, lots of people coming to visit and then a lot of people started phoning to see what help [my son] Hugh needed. He was all right – it was me that needed help trying to make sense of what was happening. Hugh went to the centre the day after the funeral and things started to get back to some routine but for a few days it was non-stop when what we needed was a bit of space for ourselves. (Personal communication)

The above example draws attention to some key points:

- It is important to be available to people and to be aware of their current situation, but it is important to ask what help is needed and when.

- It is important to be aware of any social and cultural practices that may be taking place and to be sensitive to.

- It is important to separate out thinking in terms of what the family may require help with and what the person with learning disabilities may need.

- Immediately after bereavement is not always the right time to make longer-term decisions.

- The experience of bereavement by someone with a learning disability can leave them feeling confused and wanting to be protective and loyal to other family members.

Being a focus for anxiety by others

At times of grief information may be withheld from people with learning disabilities so that they do not become too upset and there can be a general sense of exclusion from the necessary tasks involved in mourning. Illness, death and the rituals associated with loss and mourning may be shielded from people with learning disabilities because of a wish to protect but this can also result in them being excluded. Involvement during funerals is one such example.

Being dependent on others

Invariably people with learning disabilities have a greater dependency on other people to meet some of their everyday needs. This dependency can potentially make the grieving process more complex in the longer term as they recover from losing a relative or close friend.

Often there is an over-concern about 'how they will manage', or an emphasis on managing risk. These factors are essential for the safety of clients but dependency can complicate and potentially delay working through grief. The attachments that people have can be, by necessity, much stronger.

In reality, some people can appear detached when facing bereavement and change as a response to what has happened. It can be hard for others to understand as it may not be the expected reaction. Often in learning disabilities people see appropriate reactions as being 'healthy' but it is not uncommon in bereavement for a sense of disconnection to be observed.

Understanding (receptive language)

Hearing news of a death is never easy and not usually predictable. There is a possibility that we may be with the person who has died, but many deaths are communicated via hospital or care staff, other family members, or emergency services. When we hear news of a death, although we may be shocked and the words may not have sunk in, as such the words do register a finality and conceptual meaning. In effect we begin to make sense of the news and meaning even though the longer-term implications may not at first be clear.

For someone with a learning disability, this understanding may be complicated by the language used. Out of our desire to make such news less distressing, it is common to try to protect people as far as possible and the use of euphemisms can detract from the real significance of the news. This can complicate the grief process and confuse the individual concerned. Terms such as 'passed away' or 'gone' can have confusing meanings for people with limited knowledge of a situation.

To many of us facing news of a death for the first time, the language and terminology may not be familiar either. The very concept of death can be difficult to grasp, and for someone with learning disabilities this can be complicated by the desire of others not to burden the person with language that is confusing, alien or potentially frightening to them. The wish to talk around the subject rather than talk about it can lead to rather convoluted explanations that can be at best patronizing and at worst misleading.

Communication (spoken language)

The ability to communicate is central to all of us, particularly in being able to gain support around loss and bereavement. Language is often one of the difficulties facing people with learning disabilities and this can define their level of disability.

Being able to experience the feelings of loss but not articulate them in a way that communicates the depth of grief to others can be extremely distressing for people with learning disabilities. The vocabulary and language of bereavement, although sad and distressing, does just this: it allows us to communicate our grief through words and a narrative.

Having limited facility for speech and finding it hard to be understood by others can compound the central benefit of expressing loss and grief. It is common for people with learning disabilities to have few people who really understand them – maybe the ability to understand their mannerisms or speech inflections – and frequently this includes those that are closest to them such as parents. The loss of someone who understands them can be especially hard to cope with.

Cultural needs may be compromised or not met

Cultural and religious customs can define people's experience of life and death and assume a greater importance at a time of mourning for relatives and friends. Grieving can be made easier if there are the comforting rituals and familiarity of funerals and memorial services. It is not always considered appropriate to include people with learning disabilities in these rituals, although this inclusion has improved greatly in recent years. It is important not to minimize the importance of specific religious needs, particularly if these have formed a central part of a client's identity in the past.

Making existing behaviours more pronounced

The shock and subsequent stress of major change such as a bereavement or loss can result in changes in someone's behaviour as a response to their grief. With some clients who have behaviours that need a degree of support, the reality of bereavement and change can accentuate their responses. The reactions to such behaviours can depend on the consistency of staff or family who are supporting them.

For some people with learning disabilities it can be that they do not have access to ways of expressing their grief through words and so communicate their loss through verbal or physical aggression, uncharacteristic shouting or remaining silent for long periods. Clients may experience conflicting reactions from people who are caring for them and differing attitudes over the best way to help. A response to this perceived lack of control in their own lives can lead to clients expressing this through behaviours such as self-harm or eating disorders.

It is important to remember that when we are facing bereavement and major life changes, we may be able to take control of our own lives by initiating stress-reducing activities and creating the right conditions for ourselves. People with learning disabilities cannot do so in the same way.

Accentuating risk factors

A major reason why bereavement and loss can be different for learning disabled clients is the correlation with increased risk. Risk can take a number of forms and a comprehensive assessment of risk factors is a necessary part of any ongoing care. When faced with major life change, people with learning disabilities are more likely to react in a way that poses a risk to themselves. Risk assessment will involve behavioural and environmental factors. Being aware of an individual's situation and being mindful of their circumstances is an essential part of ongoing care.

As people with learning disabilities often live in shared accommodation, risk may be an issue for a number of people at the same time. The death of someone in a small residential home where people have lived together for some years and have long-term attachments may raise concerns about the impact on the other people who live there. Risk will be covered further in Chapter 4.

Access to resources

In the past people with learning disabilities had limited access to mainstream medical and social resources. Despite a gradual change in attitudes over the years, it was still relatively difficult to get access to specialist help when learning disabled clients were facing the death of family or friends. Gradual change has happened but a review was necessary to bring national services in the UK up to a common standard. John O'Brien's Five Accomplishments (1989) was a significant step towards reviewing the principles of good practice.

In 2001 the *Valuing People* White Paper built on this to increase access and covered key areas such as rights, promoting independence, choices and inclusion in community services (Department of Health 2001b). As society's discomfort and taboos around talking about death, disability, illness and dying diminished, it was significant that access for people with learning disabilities was addressed in *Valuing People* and a new framework was initiated to address these unrecognized issues. Person-centred planning approaches have built on the recent developments in enabling people to access services that are appropriate for their own needs.

With these frameworks in place, it is now easier for clients to access help when facing bereavement, loss and change. As people are often referred for help at different stages in the grief process (discussed in Chapter 4) there are further difficulties that come from services, choice and availability not always matching. This can be frustrating if you are supporting someone through grief and change.

Adoption and fostering

For some people with learning disabilities, the process of loss can begin at an early age. In the past it was common for families to place their disabled children into care. For many years, the level of support available to mothers who gave birth to children with learning disabilities was often negligible and the attitude was that it was better to put such babies into institutions.

In modern times the British Association for Adoption and Fostering has commented on the higher prevalence of adoption and fostering within learning disabilities. One of the consequences for older clients with learning disabilities who were separated from their mothers at an early age is the effect on attachments that they can subsequently make. This is another difficulty in addition to the existing disability.

Looking at clients' early histories can reveal that many young children who were placed in institutions or who were rejected by their birth mothers found it harder to form emotional bonds later in life. Missing out on the early attachments can affect a child's social and emotional development.

Many adults with learning disabilities, especially those who are now in their fifties, will have experienced this lack of holding and bonding at an early age and so are likely to find subsequent bereavements more difficult to manage.

Being treated differently

Inevitably in families there will have been ways in which someone with a learning disability has been treated differently from other family members. The initial shock of hearing the news that a child has some kind of learning disability and not knowing the outcome of their future ability and functioning will have altered the way that others approach them. It has been recognized that this communicating of difference happens consciously or unconsciously from the time that the disability is either suspected or known.

Having a family member who has a learning disability can affect communication within that family as individuals try to accommodate their needs. The expectation that people with learning disabilities will be treated differently has led to areas such as loss, death and sexuality to be approached with a hesitancy that we may not afford to others.

Assumptions being made

Assumptions can be made about 'the right way to do things' when supporting someone with learning disabilities who is facing a bereavement or major change in life. This may follow social or cultural expectations about how things are done. Stigma can complicate the area of bereavement, especially with people who can be overlooked or disempowered. It is also common for assumptions to be made based on our previous knowledge of people and how they are likely to react or respond.

When reactions are assumed we are more at risk of not respecting an individual's real wishes. It is essential to listen to what people want, to provide clear options of what is available and to advocate where necessary on behalf of those who may not be initially clear about what they want to do. Doing this in a clear but sensitive way, while still being aware of people's distress, can make the long-term adapting to a new situation much easier.

In this sense the involvement of people with learning disabilities is essential so that they can play a part in mourning and direct their grieving and adapt to a new situations. However, being dependent on others can demand that as family members and carers we go into this with an open mind and not assume what is wanted.

Lack of specific resources and training

Since the mid-1980s there has been increased interest in how to effectively support people with learning disabilities around loss, grief and change. There has also been a greater development in accessible training tools and help for carers and agencies. However, specialist training often comes at a cost, training budgets are limited and staff turnover can increase at times of change within an organization. There can be issues depending on the political climate of the time whether support can be given for bereavement training and resources may be scarce.

On a systemic and interpersonal level, not having access to specific knowledge and training can create problems especially if there is a sudden and unexpected death within a residential home, where staff can feel overwhelmed while facing the reality of the situation and waiting for support and training. This inevitably leads to more stress for everyone involved with the home.

Variety of carers and lack of intimate relationships following bereavement

Often if there is a sudden bereavement or change in circumstances, learning disabled clients can be required to move so that they can be cared for. When a main caregiver dies or has to receive care themselves, it means that the client concerned could face a period where they are being cared for by several people who will have only limited amount of contact with them due to shift patterns. It is hard in such situations to form intimate relationships with people in a short space of time.

Longer processing over period of time

One specific difference for people with learning disabilities who experience bereavement is that the event itself often leads to many other life changes. If the individual requires respite care, as well as facing the shock of what has happened, there are other practical and immediate changes. This can be very disorientating for many individuals.

A funeral may signify a kind of marker in the process of grief followed by a return to a routine. This superficial 'back to normal' feeling that can often bring some relief may mask the fact that processing grief can take a much longer period. For people with learning disabilities, this processing can be more complicated depending on the degree of their disability, what their situation was before the bereavement and then after it.

Effects on existing mental health issues

Having a learning disability predisposes people to a number of psychological, social and biological factors that can impact on their mental health. These can ultimately make clients more vulnerable at key times of change and stress, including bereavement. When someone close to a person with a learning disability dies, there is an increased risk that their mental health will be affected.

Access to specialist services and assessment may be limited depending on where the person lives and depending on referral networks. It can also be hard to assess when what might be a normal grief reaction has the potential to impact on someone's mental health.

Medication

There have been general improvements in the monitoring and administration of medications for physical and mental health problems that can occur more readily in the learning disability population. A major shock or life change such as bereavement can result in a potential imbalance where the emotional reaction to shock may make a person vulnerable. Closer monitoring is required of how people react to life change so that this vulnerability is reduced. Talking therapy, one intervention that may be offered at some point following a bereavement or loss, would have to take into account how this may impact on an individual and it is necessary to check any contraindications.

Feeling 'different' and being treated differently

Any bereavement or significant negative life event can make us feel vulnerable if support is not available in the right way. The sense of isolation that accompanies bereavement can remind someone of their learning disability and of their vulnerability and increased dependence on others.

Times of bereavement can not only be stressful but also remind individuals of being an outsider or maybe tap into impressions of being excluded or not wanted. Support is very important at these times and if it is not available it can make someone more vulnerable to further problems at least in the short to medium term.

Difficult or stressful to piece together a narrative

In accepting or coming to terms with bereavement, part of the way that one can cope is to achieve the many tasks and stages that are associated with the grief process. Part of this is to be able to build a perspective of a period of time in the past that has now gone or a making sense of a difficult time that preceded someone's death if there has been pain or suffering. Gaining a perspective can involve comparing previous losses with the current one or looking for ways that one coped previously.

As learning disability affects the process of learning and being able to recall events and facts from the past, building up a narrative or story of the experience of what someone has gone through can be much more difficult. The order of life events and life history can be confused, especially if the person involved spent part of their life being comparatively passive in decisions. When thinking back about someone or a part of their lives, people with learning disabilities may not have the same wealth of memories and this also affects the way that they grieve.

Change in identity

A major consequence of any bereavement is how it leaves the grieving person's sense of their own identity. Historically the way that people's identity has been formed and maintained when they have had any kind of disability has been subject to the way that other people see them and the projections that are put on to them by others.

The way that someone views themselves comes into greater focus at times of bereavement, especially if the person who has now died was responsible for making them view themselves in the way that they do. Low self-esteem is invariably the consequence of not feeling included or the fear of rejection. If this has been the experience of someone with a learning disability, a bereavement can leave ambivalent feelings of anger and guilt as well as loss towards the person who has died. The subsequent reframing of identity and how the person with learning disabilities sees themselves can be a major issue following bereavement.

Stigma

It could be said that the stigma that is often attached to people with learning disabilities is such that beliefs are unconsciously held about their exposure to loss. People can make huge efforts to protect the person with learning disabilities from loss in the misplaced belief that they will not be able to hold its emotional reality.

Hollins (1995) states that:

> strenuous efforts are often made to protect people with intellectual disabilities from life's losses and disappointments. The harsh reality of their own and their parents' mortality is a secret they will have been judged too vulnerable to be told. Their death education has often been non-existent, so their bewilderment at the disappearance of a loved one should be no surprise.

The process of withholding information, avoiding the truth and stigmatizing a whole section of society can lead to it being more difficult to progress, and the avoidance of things that require careful thinking.

Isolation

Increasingly due to changes in lifestyle, health and social policy and the focus on independent living, a significant number of people with learning disabilities are living on their own. Some have done so by choice while others have managed to stay on in properties where they lived with parents or family and they now live in on their own.

The emphasis on independent living, changes in the benefits system and schemes such as direct payments have enabled people to have a greater control over their own lives than before.

The change in the role of day services and financial changes in the UK means that an increasing number of people have a more flexible structure for part of their lives. In the US, Canada and Australia, services for people with developmental disabilities are organized by the individual states. When facing a bereavement, this can become very isolating especially if individuals are not actively known or involved with services. It can be easy for someone's distress and need for some support to go unnoticed. Therefore one of the risks for people with learning disabilities who are facing bereavement (and the subsequent depression which often accompanies it) is that there can be isolation.

Historically having a learning disability has involved a lived experience of separateness for many people. This may have begun at birth when special care had to be given in order to protect life or, some years ago, the advice that there was 'nothing that could be done'. Nowadays there is a greater emphasis on recognizing potential and assessing at different ages to ensure that children who have disabilities can achieve their maximum potential. The experience of separation has diminished as society's attitudes towards all aspects of disability have become less critical but the legacy of this is still a sense of separateness that many clients and families carry on some level.

Self-blame

In the absence of any concrete understanding of or reason why people die, someone with learning disabilities may think that it is their fault that the person they loved has died. This can be common if there has been little exposure to death and if the relationship that they have had with the deceased person has been very close and intimate. It may seem as if there is no one else to blame. If grieving is predominantly experienced alone, then there is less opportunity to balance the thinking of the grieving person and so this can reinforce the feeling that people are alone.

Self-blame can come from a feeling of disempowerment but often people with learning disabilities are powerless to effect change and find it hard to help or take an active role in a constructive way. Situations surrounding illness and death can accentuate the feeling that 'I should have done more'.

Case study: Ashwin

Ashwin attended a day centre for three days a week, always on Monday, Tuesday and Friday. He lived with his mum, who was in her eighties and went to an older persons' centre on Mondays and Fridays. When his mum had a stroke one Tuesday, she was admitted to a stroke and rehabilitation ward for five weeks. When Ashwin was on his own, he became fixed on the fact that it had been on a Tuesday and that 'if it had been on a Wednesday she would have been all right because I would have been there and I could have stopped it'.

It took him several months to begin to let go of this guilt and to recognize that it wasn't his fault. A few months later he heard an advert on the TV about what to do if someone has a stroke and this brought the anxiety back for him again. It was only his mum talking to him about it and a subsequent visit to his general practitioner (GP) to give him some reassurance that helped him to let go of the anxiety around it.

The above case example illustrates how it can be difficult to work with the fixed beliefs that clients have around what they could or should have done, when often it is out of their hands.

Not knowing when grieving 'stops' following bereavement

It can be hard for many people to make sense of what happens during any loss experience. There can often be very few cues that tell us that now is the time to recover and what is appropriate and when it should happen.

People with learning disabilities can have limited experience and some fantasies of what bereavement involves if they have not had much exposure to it. Staff may be absent because of a personal bereavement and not be at work for a few days. Because our society still tends to keep bereavement hidden, ideas can become distorted about what the process of death and dying are about if one has had limited exposure to it.

Television soap operas are a good example of unrealistic portrayals of grief. Within a few episodes one can have an illness, death, a funeral and within weeks the bereaved character can be getting back into a routine and the grief is apparently forgotten about.

Key points from this chapter

- Bereavement can be another massive rejection if an individual has already had some difficult loss around their early attachments. It is not always possible for individuals to utilize resources from their own previous learning to apply as strategies for new situations.

- Bereavement can reawaken past personal history in someone's life that can be difficult to manage. People with learning disabilities can have complex early histories that involve trauma, separation, illness and not being listened to and these inevitably complicate the way that they can manage when facing further loss.

- People who have experienced a lot of isolation and rejection can find it hard to trust professionals who are there to help and are likely to have had negative experiences of such relationships in the past. This can have implications for someone's engagement with services.

3

Stages of Loss

Introduction

In understanding the process of mourning and loss following a bereavement, writers and therapists often refer to loss as being in stages. It is recognized that loss, including bereavement, can be experienced in stages that are worked through. This can indicate that the process of loss has a beginning and an end; to some extent, this is true. However, the experience of bereavement is not necessarily sequential where one phase and feeling leads to another in an orderly and convenient way.

The first year following a major bereavement or loss can be the most difficult. The experience of different emotions and being out of control of what actually happens in one's own life can make this experience much more complicated for people with learning disabilities, their families and carers. It can feel that change is overwhelming. However, the process of loss that accompanies a bereavement or major life change does not happen immediately.

Viewing the loss process as being in stages was first identified by Elisabeth Kübler-Ross (1970). William Worden (2003) and other writers have also used a stages and tasks model to give an overview of grief and loss as being a process.

This chapter describes what many people consider to be the main stages of loss. The stages outlined do not necessarily follow in a particular order or be apparent for everyone.

Shock

The first reaction to hearing the news of a death is shock. This is often dependent on the type of death that someone has heard about and is more common if the death is sudden and unexpected. The manner in which one finds out about a death can be a major contributing factor as to how one manages in the immediate aftermath of hearing the news. If someone has been ill for some time and then dies, there is often a degree of shock but it is less so if it has been expected. If someone with learning disabilities experiences shock at the news of a death, this has to be managed carefully.

Denial

It is common when people hear news of a death that they want to 'not believe' the news. People often say they 'can't believe it'. Denial is an instinctive response to the impact of a loss. It is as if the news is so sudden or so shocking that we block out the fact and the feeling that goes with it. This blocking of feeling is often described as being 'numb'. Rather than bringing the news into consciousness and being aware of it, the body and mind block it out to protect against the flood of grief that we fear may overwhelm us.

People with learning disabilities can take longer to make sense of information, due to cognitive or emotional factors, and so denial can be a more serious part of the grief process. Finding it hard to accept the change that bereavement brings can result in new behaviours and reactions. It can also exaggerate any existing behavioural difficulties that someone has.

Bargaining

Having heard sad news and not wanting to believe it, our reaction can be to push the truth away and try to convince ourselves that nothing has happened. This can be especially true if the person we have lost has died somewhere away from where we are.

Some people try to make a deal with themselves at this stage, perhaps pretending that nothing has happened so that everything will seem as if it is normal and there has been no change. Some people attempt to make a deal between themselves and a higher power in the face of irreversible change such as 'If I promise to be good from this point onwards then maybe the consequences of the loss won't be the same'.

It can take a long time for some people to begin to accept the reality of their loss and to begin to let go of all the strategies that they have used to deny the finality of change. In the area of learning disabilities this may take the form of recognizing that someone they love will not actually come back, or that a move to a different home from their family home is not just a holiday but likely to be permanent.

There can be a real ambivalence to taking in the news of someone's death. People with learning disabilities may have heard the news via someone else and there is likely to be some mixed feelings around for whoever tells the person what has happened.

Searching

Searching is often described as being a stage in the loss process where having not fully accepted the reality of the loss one has experienced, there is a continuing process of looking for the person who is lost. This can be expressed in searching for a new person to become attached to who might be able to replace some of the qualities that the deceased person gave. Often after a bereavement people with learning disabilities can either become distant or appear to wish to spend more time with staff. This is because of the desire or search for replacing aspects of the person that they have lost.

Searching can be quite an emotionally painful process as it can lead to stress and can postpone the realization that, in spite of trying hard to replicate the lost relationship, the deceased person is not coming back. Searching can precede or accompany anxiety as one struggles to understand what has happened.

Anxiety

William Worden, a writer on bereavement and loss, has stated that 'anxiety relates to a heightened sense of personal death awareness – the awareness of one's own mortality heightened by the death of a loved one' (Worden 2003, p.13). It is true that people with learning disabilities also experience a higher degree of anxiety and worry when there is major change around. This can be because events can seem to be happening outside of their control and specific life events such as illness, loss and death can inevitably leave people feeling powerless to effect change.

Fear of the consequences after someone has gone may have been held for years or when other people have been observed not coping well when a carer or parent has died. The reliance on a parent or carer can be very strong and the anxiety felt by separation can be very acute.

Following bereavement it is common for us to experience a heightened sense of our own mortality. It is common to feel vulnerable at this stage and to carry anxieties about our own health. Experiencing bereavement can be very frightening in this way, especially if it is the first time that someone with learning disabilities has experienced separation.

Anger

It is understandable to feel angry during bereavement. Anger can often follow the death of someone close. The individual can feel anger against the person for leaving them alone, particularly if the death is sudden. For people with learning disabilities, it can seem as if the person who they thought was going to be there for years has left them and it feels very unfair.

A common reaction is to get angry with people around them, especially with family or staff who have to maintain some boundaries in their lives. Getting back to a routine following a funeral or loss can bring up feelings of intense anger for some people, who feel as if it is almost as if those around them haven't noticed the extent of their grief or want to push them back to a centre or activity before they feel ready.

Anger can be turned inwards following bereavement and not expressed so openly, taking the form of stress and depression. It is a challenge of bereavement and loss to work with this in a way that helps people recognize how and why they get angry. If anger can be expressed or turned into something that people can use constructively, it can be more beneficial. In environments where anger has to be 'managed' and where people may have anger management strategies to help them, it is important to be as sensitive as possible following bereavement.

Guilt

People often have feelings of guilt following a bereavement. This can be based on regret that they did not do certain things when someone was alive or failed to prevent negative things from happening. It has to be recognized that guilt is an area that can be felt but often not talked about by parents of people with disabilities and that this can be rooted in feelings of helplessness. This can become part of the experience of mourning following a loss or major change.

Another manifestation of this is the concept of 'survivor guilt' following a bereavement where the person left behind can question why they are still here. It can take a long time for feelings around this to be recognized and talked through.

In the context of learning disabilities, this can be part of the unexpressed experience of people living in residential services where people can be witness to other people's illness but feel powerless to effect any change on their behalf.

There can be some powerful and psychologically destructive connections between shame, not being able to assume control over a situation such as bereavement, and feeling that one has let oneself down or not been good enough at times of bereavement. This can be overlooked for those with learning disabilities.

Depression

Depressive feelings are very common following a bereavement and can last for a long time, especially if the loss has been complicated by other factors such as having to move or feeling powerless to make changes in one's life. Depression can follow an initial bereavement or life change and then recur at times of anniversaries. It can last for a significant period of time depending on how it is managed.

Depression is characterized by many features such as having a low mood that does not lift for some time, feeling lonely and sad, losing energy and motivation, and experiencing social withdrawal. Depression can be the result of something that has happened, sometimes called reactive depression.

In learning disabilities, depression can be complicated by a number of factors including communication difficulties, behavioural change and misunderstandings of others. If clients cannot say why they feel as they do, then being aware of their physical and psychological well-being is very important.

Depression can potentially be serious and can hold people back from moving on from bereavement. If it does not improve then it is important to get some guidance about how to manage it. A period of feeling low frequently accompanies the time after bereavement. If it persists and does not improve, this is when depression becomes more of a potential difficulty and will mean that help has to be sought from a general practitioner (GP) or mental health practitioner. Depression is a normal reaction to bereavement and loss yet it can be serious and needs treatment if it persists.

Grief and mourning

The writer Colin Murray Parkes (1972, p.26) states that 'Grief is the price we pay for love'. The onset of grief in the bereavement process occurs when the previous stages have been touched upon and the loss of relationship is realized.

It is usual and necessary to experience a period of mourning following bereavement. The feelings of loss and sadness that accompany this can last for some weeks or months. As time moves on these feelings and reactions usually subside as the individual becomes more used to the new situation. Days of sadness and feeling low still come in the time after the bereavement. To mourn is to recognize the significance of our loss. Culturally we recognize this when we have to face bereavement.

People with learning disabilities are more likely to have so-called 'complex grief' due to the greater likelihood that their needs can be overlooked and their place in a family or society can be thrown into focus at such times. However, there is no inevitability to this and the grief and mourning experienced by many is more likely to be a usual life event that can be helped by the support of others.

Maureen Oswin in her book *Am I Allowed to Cry?* comments that staff working with people with learning disabilities may not recognize that grieving is a normal reaction to a death or loss because 'staff may be inexperienced in their knowledge of bereavement or because their approach to a person with a learning disability concentrates on abnormality rather than normality' (Oswin 1991, p.27).

It takes time to go through the routines associated with bereavement and this can often be managed in a way that does not require any specialist help. Supporting an individual, regardless of whether they have a disability or not, can be all that is needed.

Acceptance

This is the final stage in the loss process and indicates a time when someone has resolved most of the stages of grief and mourning. It has been possible to express the feelings of loss and to accept what has happened as being irreversible. Routines are often back in place and people find that they can talk about the person who died or the change that happened with a degree of perspective. It is at this stage that people do not get upset by talking about it.

Acceptance can involve reflective thinking about different losses. Building up a perspective of these losses and seeing their meaning or significance to someone can indicate that the stages of loss have been successfully managed.

How we can help this process

The stages of bereavement are not necessarily sequential and do not follow in a convenient pattern with a start and an end. The first few months are likely to be the most difficult for someone who has experienced bereavement. It is important to remember that bereavement is a process. It may lead to other practical and psychological difficulties or exaggerate existing behavioural difficulties, but it does eventually find some kind of resolution.

It has to be emphasized at this point that the stages of loss are not literal: they are a way to describe the psychological process that people experience following a bereavement or loss. If you are supporting someone through bereavement and subsequent change, the following points are relevant in terms of thinking about the process of bereavement.

Not giving false hope

It can be tempting to reassure someone in distress following bereavement in order to minimize their reactions. Sometimes it can be hard to be around someone who is obviously grieving. Giving false hope at this stage to make them feel 'better' can be unhelpful. It is better to acknowledge the loss, reassure but not say that 'everything will be all right' if it is clear that this may not be so.

Being supportive and consistent – especially in staff teams

Being consistent is important following bereavement and loss, but this can be difficult in situations where there is a lot of change. It is helpful to have clear explanations of who is going to be available or on shift in residential services.

In other services it is important that people are informed of who is working when, so that there is some consistency. Having a policy that is consistent but that can be adapted to meet the needs of individuals can give a very clear message to others about the way that care can be given at such times.

Recognizing the range of emotions that follow bereavement

The stages in a grief reaction are often accompanied by strong emotions, some of which are voiced or enacted and others which are repressed. Being accepting of this can help us to support people when they are distressed. Of course sometimes these emotions can be hard to manage, especially where people feel exposed or vulnerable.

Being clear in the language used

The language that we use when communicating the reality of a loss or bereavement to someone with a learning disability has to be not only clear and unambiguous but also sensitive. Some people with learning disabilities see things in quite a matter of fact way but it is important not to respond with the same bluntness. While not holding back the truth, the way that we respond can communicate something about the way we value the person's experience and what they are facing.

Recognizing unique circumstances – not like a soap opera

Everyone's experience of bereavement is different and reactions to it will depend on previous loss, behavioural reactions and how clients typically express themselves. As such everyone's experience is unique. It is often a surprise to people with learning disabilities that their experiences around this are different from how they imagined.

Death can be realistically portrayed on television soap operas in the immediate storylines, for example, but often grief reactions are not followed through. Clients' unique situations often do not conform to the stereotypes that are acted out on the screen. Soaps can be a useful topic in discussion generally in social education groups but cannot then translate into people's own experience.

Seeing things from the client's point of view

When supporting someone after a bereavement, seeing things from the client's view is essential. It is common to have to advocate for someone with a learning disability following bereavement. This may involve supporting them to take part in the mourning process or talking with them at different times through the subsequent weeks and months. At all times even if we disagree with some of the things that are said, it is important to be able to see a situation from their point of view. Doing so will have the effect of clients being more likely to feel supported.

Keeping clear boundaries

As the bereavement process takes its course, it is important to be supportive and not to dwell on what has happened too much with clients. Talking can help, but keeping active and doing things is part of the support. If a client you are working with initiates talking about their bereavement, it is important to be available to talk to them. However, do not assume that people want to talk about it every time you work with them. Keeping a routine and maintaining the boundaries between yourself and the person you are caring for enables the stages of loss to be worked through more clearly.

Recognizing that it is possible to live without the person who has died

When people face bereavement or change that involves separation, such as living on their own for the first time, it can highlight the dependency that they feel. It is common to think 'I can't cope'. Helping someone after bereavement involves assessing what skills people have. If a parent was someone who did everything previously, then it can be hard to alter routines to help individuals to live as independently as possible.

Accepting that loss and mourning present in many forms

The way that loss and the process of mourning affect people with learning disabilities is different from person to person and is unique to them. Some people may not appear to be as affected by bereavement and the changes that accompany it as others. This raises the question: What is a 'normal' grief reaction? Each person's situation and ability to adapt and cope with change is different and will depend on the context in which the bereavement is experienced. It is, perhaps, the consistency of people who support someone with a learning disability that is most important. The complications of having different attitudes from others when facing bereavement and loss can be confusing and we have to recognize that people mourn in individual ways.

Recognizing the link between anxiety as a trigger for behavioural reactions

There is often an increase in challenging behaviour for people with learning disabilities following loss, especially for clients with limited language skills. In loss terms this would be seen as a response to separation. In many ways it is an understandable response as the security afforded by the caregiver (or the person who cared for someone in the past) has departed and the attachment has now gone.

Holmes (1993) describes the anxiety that separation can bring as 'a subjective feeling of worry, pain and tension; angry protest, whose function is to register displeasure and to punish the errant partner…a restless searching for the missing person' (Holmes 1993, p.89).

John Bowlby, a psychoanalyst who developed attachment theory, stated that bereavement reaction is an irreversible form of separation (Holmes 1993). In working with adults who find it hard to communicate their distress following loss, bereavement and change, it is important to recognize that too much change too soon can be devastating.

Careful planning following a bereavement that has led to further losses has to take account of the strength of feeling associated with separation. It is true that this separation is in fact irreversible. As carers, families and professionals working with people with learning disabilities, we have a responsibility to try to ease the impact of that separation but we cannot prevent it from happening.

Key points from this chapter

- Bereavement and other losses that are a consequence of it, such as moving house, separation and changes in routine, can be especially difficult and confusing for people that we work with, often leading to changes in health and behaviour.

- There are specific things that we can do to support clients through the bereavement process. Being aware of the different stages of a bereavement reaction and being supportive to people as and when necessary is important.

- It is helpful to draw upon the help of other professionals where necessary to assist in the bereavement process, being aware of an individual's cultural, spiritual and religious beliefs and needs. Setting up relevant training and supervision is another aspect of this.

4

Assessment

Introduction

This chapter highlights the importance of assessment when working with clients who are anticipating or experiencing bereavement. Assessing risk is a crucial concern for people with learning disabilities in order to minimize physical and psychological harm. Its purpose is to facilitate and ease change facing people who are essentially in transition.

During a major life change, we often have to draw upon our own physical, spiritual and psychological resources as well as the support of wider family and friends. This supposes that there are people in our lives who can do this.

Having such support helps us to foster resilience in the face of unexpected change. The degree to which adults with learning disabilities have access to such support can be limited, and can add to existing vulnerabilities and risk factors as they struggle to make sense of what has happened and its meaning.

Being faced with bereavement and major change can maximize existing risk factors for someone. It is understandable to feel vulnerable and confused when faced with bereavement, especially in the first few weeks. This can add to the existing perceived risks.

Some psychological risks may appear over a longer period of time and may be the point at which the specific difficulties for learning disabled clients become more apparent. There is also a role for practitioners in assessing practical and emotional risks to the client and others.

This chapter considers two different areas where assessment is essential for clients: first, risk assessment focusing on the risks posed as a consequence of the change bereavement or loss bring, and second, the factors to consider when assessing a client for talking therapy. The factors that increase risk are also noted and how risk can be identified and managed within the therapeutic framework.

Background to risk

There is now a comprehensive framework within which to manage situations that pose risk to people with learning disabilities. In the past risk was managed in a less joined-up way that did not reflect the reality of people's lives. Introducing the Care Programme Approach (CPA) in the UK meant that there was greater coordination in the thinking around how the mental health needs of people with learning disabilities are managed for individuals. The CPA is a central part of the care management process for people with mental health problems who come in to services. Involving people with learning disabilities in this assessment scheme, under a standard or enhanced level depending on their presenting need, it is a way of managing potential and actual risks to individuals.

The *Valuing People* White Paper enabled a modernizing of services that people with learning disabilities had access to and focused on inclusion, choice, rights and gaining and maintaining independence as key goals for everyone (Department of Health 2001b).

In the UK, general practitioners (GPs) have a central role in the lives of people with learning disabilities, but services are provided by Community Learning Disabilities teams, Community Mental Health teams and teams that address the specific needs of people who have joint mental health and learning disabilities. Prior to *Valuing People* in 2001, there had not been any major policy change for about 30 years. During that time the lives and opportunities of people with learning disabilities – and their exposure to bereavement and change – changed massively.

If people need care as inpatients following a crisis or concern about their mental health, it is now possible to be treated in a hospital ward that is more likely to address their mental health while recognizing their additional learning disabilities.

By making treatment in line with the principles of person-centred-planning, people who access treatment can do so in a way that puts them at the centre of the process. This goes a long way to address the negative historical legacy of the past.

Bereavement and major life change can have a direct impact on the mental health of people with learning disabilities. Care has to be taken to ensure that there is a plan in place to manage risk and to ensure the individual's safety and support.

Both the CPA process and *Valuing People* initiative have meant that the impact of any mental health decline following such life events can be more effectively managed for individuals. In addition the CPA review meetings can track the way that individuals are managing and evaluate any presenting risks.

Care plans

There are two different levels of risk covered by the CPA: 'standard' and 'enhanced'. These reflect the level of support felt necessary to be put in place to ensure someone's safety. In the US the American Psychiatric Association's Diagnostic and Statistical Manual of Mental Disorders provides a framework for risk. In Australia Einfield and Tonge devised The Developmental Behaviour Checklist to assess risk.

Some bereavements will result in individuals facing significant change in their lives. This raises their vulnerability to mental health problems. If these are felt to be more serious, then they will be more likely to be placed on 'enhanced' CPA plans.

The CPA ensures that everyone deemed to have any risk factors to their mental health can be assessed by a mental health professional. Following this, each individual is given a care plan to state how their health and social care needs are met and how these services are provided.

Each person has access to a 'care coordinator', who can be a point of reference at care plan meetings and at any points of difficulty. He or she can then arrange regular reviews as necessary where the individual, their carers, an allocated community psychiatric nurse and psychiatrist can all attend.

Managing greater risks posed to the individual

Bereavement can place people in a heightened state of anxiety and grief. For some clients the unthinkable may have actually come true where they have lost the person who not only loved them from birth but also provided for most of their needs. The shock of losing such an important person can push people into a very vulnerable place which, even if it is temporary, has to be taken seriously.

The risk that individuals may attempt to take their own life or otherwise harm themselves is seen as being greater at times of extreme stress. It is one of the main assessment points of the CORE assessment tool and should be picked up by those involved in an individual's care. The Core assessment tool is a way of assessing the mental health of clients who are referred and may be at risk of developing depression. It is used widely to assess risk around mood and behaviour in people who have learning disabilities. Thinking ahead by professionals can help to limit this risk by anticipating it. In terms of strategic thinking across the mental health services in the UK, the National Framework for Mental Health has made reducing suicide rates one of its key standards for progress. The National Service Frameworks set a uniform standard of national health care to be expected across the health sector in the UK and draw upon the best available evidence for conditions.

If someone you care for is talking about wanting to end their own life, it is important to alert services. If there is no care plan in place, then contact the senior management in the team you work for. If you are caring for someone on your own outside of an established service, request help either from the medical profesional involved in the individual's care or NHS Direct in the UK.

Relevance to bereavement and loss

The above strategies are relevant to what happens when an individual experiences bereavement and loss as they provide a framework within which a person's situation can be assessed. As depression and behaviour change can often be a consequence of managing the altered situation that follows bereavement, it is necessary to have a system that contains the risks posed.

Facing any bereavement or loss can increase the risk around an individual with learning disabilities. The following points are worth bearing in mind when assessing this:

- Was the bereavement or loss preceded by a period of uncertainty and/or instability? Examples of this could be, for example, the deteriorating health of a carer or a decline in the degree of self care.
- Has there been a noticeable change in the way that the individual relates to others following a bereavement or loss?

- Has there been a necessary change in accommodation and/or care arrangements following a bereavement which there has not been adequate time to prepare for?

- Has any physical, psychological or sexual abuse been revealed following the bereavement or loss and is there still a potential for this abuse?

- Following a bereavement is there potential for financial abuse to take place?

If any of the above points present as being risks, then the appropriate risk procedures should be put in place as part of the CPA. As a carer it is important to be aware of the need for transparency to ensure that a situation remains safe for the individual concerned.

Depression

People with learning disabilities are just as likely to get depressed as anyone else. How this shows itself can be different, especially if they feel unable to put into words how they feel. It is usual for someone who is bereaved to appear to be in low mood and have elements of reactive depression following a loss or bereavement. It is recognized as being part of the consequence of losing something or someone close and can evoke feelings of helplessness and isolation. In learning disabilities the signs of depression may be masked or less obvious. These may include a loss of interest in things usually enjoyed and a noticeable loss of energy and activity levels. Feeling tired all the time can be a sign of depression.

Some people report that they think life is not worth living when they are particularly unhappy. This requires careful risk assessment and it is essential that not only are these ideas explored but also the person is taken seriously. Parents or carers are in the best position to notice these changes in the person they are caring for. The parent or carer may have experienced this bereavement directly as well as the person cared for, and may be coping with their own feelings following what has happened. Another complicating factor can be if the individual concerned has had to move in addition to coping with the grief. A delayed reaction of depression is more common in these situations. If things are not getting any better, this is when an assessment can help.

People who live on their own and have minimal contact with services are likely to be at most risk. A number of professionals including social work, occupational therapy and mental health may be involved at this time. The following points can indicate if someone might be depressed and are likely to be picked up in an assessment of need.

Behaviour changes such as anxiety and panic

Anxiety is often shown by people becoming more dependent on others who are around them, particularly new or temporary carers, for example in respite care. Staff often find that individuals who are staying at a respite unit following a death are anxious and cling to them for support, especially if they know the staff members from before. It is common for people to be forgetful, maybe through anxiety and being preoccupied following bereavement. This is usually temporary and will lessen as a situation improves.

Changes in bowel and bladder control can be indications of current anxiety that require some kind of monitoring as it can be distressing for individuals, especially if they associate it with shame around old behaviours.

Sleep pattern changes that persist

It is usual for patterns of sleep to be disrupted following loss and change. It can indicate a continuing anxiety and is a further factor indicating some depression. Sleep is an important indicator of how anxiety and adjustment are being managed. Keeping a sleep diary can be helpful in identifying patterns of sleep disturbance.

Finding it hard to get off to sleep at night and waking early in the morning are signs that indicate sleep disturbance; if this is unusual for someone and is linked to a bereavement or loss, it is important to consider. Asking how long there have been sleep problems as well as asking about sleep patterns and quality can indicate how individuals are coping.

Some people appear to sleep for much longer than before. This should be monitored as it could indicate underlying physical or psychological issues.

Some people with learning disabilities who are in relationships find that being alone without their partner can be hard to get used to. Changes in environment can also have a large effect (the room, temperature, light and so on).

Anger

Changes can be indicated when people show anger or challenging behaviour. The link between this and self-harm is clear, because if the anger is turned in on oneself, self-injury can follow. Self-harm can be associated with a frustration with not being able to communicate. If people you are working with show this as a way of expressing anger, it is advisable to find other ways of channelling their anger. Chapter 9 on non-verbal communication may offer some therapeutic ways that anger can be expressed.

It is worth thinking about what the anger may mean in the context of the individual's loss when doing an assessment in learning disabilities, as well as the inevitable risk that may be posed if the anger turns to a more physically violent expression of grief. Being snappy and irritable may be less physical, but should also be seen as manifestations of grief and anger that are usually short term.

Physical manifestations of grief

Physical manifestations of grief occur frequently when something cannot be expressed in terms of repressed feelings. There can be times when people with learning disabilities are left with anger following a loss or death that they cannot communicate in words. One woman said about her mother: 'I hated her, I hated her – I wanted to punch her in the stomach'. This action never actually happened but the individual concerned had a series of undiagnosed stomach complaints that led to surgery a couple of years later.

Feelings of illness

It is common for people with learning disabilities to say that they are feeling ill or unwell following times of bereavement, loss, stress or uncertainty around the future. Obviously if someone is displaying physical symptoms that are immediate or urgent, medical help should be sought. However, it is generally recognized that grief that is not directly expressed can have behavioural or physical symptoms. This may be more common in people with learning disabilities, who often do not have the language or vocabulary to say in words how they are feeling.

Colin Murray Parkes explores these reactions and states: 'Persons who do not allow themselves to experience grief directly may develop medical symptoms similar to those which the deceased displayed or they may develop some other kind of psychosomatic complaint' (Parkes 1972, p.94).

The following physical symptoms often accompany grief:

- constantly feeling nauseous, but never being sick
- having a tightness in the throat
- feeling faint
- feeling weak and having no energy
- being oversensitive to noise.

It is important that any physical symptoms are monitored and taken seriously, especially in a residential setting where there is a constant handover of staff, in order to get a continuous picture of someone's health.

Assessing this will involve monitoring routines and moods of an individual client. Although these are often referred to and also dismissed as being 'psychosomatic' in nature, particularly in the general population, it is important to listen to any changes in health that people with learning disabilities report.

Eating and drinking

It is common for people to go off their food following a bereavement or change. Any change can create stress, and stress is a big factor in dietary change. Some people 'comfort eat' when they are stressed or feeling low, whereas others find that they lose their appetite when coping with grief.

Changes in eating and drinking may indicate distress that is temporary, although any changes in weight or eating patterns or habits should be monitored in case of further complications. Some people with learning disabilities may have conditions such as diabetes diagnosed only after a visit to the GP following a period of stress or when they visit a new GP, having moved house. Changes in diet and eating habits can indicate problems following an assessment.

There are behavioural aspects to changes in eating following a loss, particularly when moving to live with other people. These can be an indication of emotional distress and should again be taken seriously.

Self-esteem

It is common for confidence and self-esteem to be affected by loss. As well as a loss of confidence, many individuals who have had to cope with change often require extra reassurance. If this has followed the death of someone that they felt very close to, it may also be accompanied by a withdrawal as if the trust cannot be replicated with anyone else. Developing a trusting relationship with others may take time as will the confidence to be in social situations. Social anxiety can often follow a major life change for people with learning disabilities as they begin to adapt to new surroundings in new unfamiliar situations.

Change and loss can leave feelings of guilt or worthlessness in individuals with learning disabilities. The world can become an unfamiliar often fearful place when change has not been on one's own terms. It can take time to get to know new people and this can also be difficult in terms of how one sees oneself. Assessing how individuals are adapting to change in these situations is crucial in their ultimate success or failure.

Assessment of behaviours that may be seen as attention seeking

Other assessments can involve working with behaviours that may in other circumstances be viewed as attention seeking or a cry for help. Stealing from local shops is a behaviour that indicates distress. Gambling is another. Although seen more in the general population, there is a link between gambling and stress that reflects a compulsion and restlessness that can also be found in times of loss.

More typically, people with learning disabilities may show wandering behaviours as if searching for someone or something following bereavement. This risk factor will need to be assessed if an individual is likely to get lost. It can also be seen in some individuals as a difficulty in being able to relax and a kind of restlessness.

Factors to consider when assessing for any therapeutic work

In assessing for any counselling or therapy work, the following factors should be taken into consideration.

Circumstances of the bereavement

The circumstances of a bereavement or loss can give an indication of the best course of intervention for someone with learning disabilities. This will suggest what services should be involved and whether joint working is necessary to facilitate the best outcome for the individual concerned. For example, both talking therapy and speech therapy may be the most helpful ways of enabling someone to communicate their loss. If someone has had to move following a bereavement, joint working between psychology and occupational therapy could be the most helpful. Following a bereavement, however, it is advisable not to overload the client with services.

The following questions are among those that are frequently considered when assessing following bereavement, and may follow assessment if a loss or bereavement was anticipated:

- Was the bereavement expected or sudden?
- Was there any planning or preparation prior to the bereavement?
- Has the individual had to move following the bereavement?
- What existing social support is in place for the individual?

Suitability for therapeutic work

In any therapeutic intervention there is a need for assessment. To know the focus of the work and the presenting state of a client is essential for its effectiveness. Talking therapy is, on the whole, dependent on an assessment of how receptive someone will be to working on the impact of the loss and their receptiveness to engaging in a therapeutic relationship. The assessment is focused on current functioning, risk and management, and talking therapy may be one of a number of options that are available to help someone.

Readiness

When assessing for counselling it is important to think about whether a referral has been made at the right time. It is usual to experience feelings of grief and sadness after bereavement and to factor this in around the thinking about whether or not now is the right time to refer someone for sessions. Facts to consider are the circumstances of the death, how much initial understanding is present, and whether therapeutic work will impact on someone's wider psychological health.

It is sometimes expected that people will cope badly following bereavement because of preconceived views of the individual concerned, when actually they have been managing well.

Usually bereavement referrals should allow time for the initial stages of grief to pass. It is important to see how the individual client copes. If there are other disruptions to their lives following a death, such as moving home, it can be better to wait until this is complete before making a referral to counselling.

Sometimes referrals are made as others need to feel that they are doing something. It can be hard to sit with other people's distress but referrals have to be made with the consent of the individual concerned and there has to be some understanding from the individual about how this can help and that they want to talk to someone from outside their usual contacts.

Typically counselling or psychological therapy can begin a couple of months after bereavement, which allows the individual's situation to have settled a bit. People who are living alone may find one-to-one work helpful sooner than this.

Consent

Before beginning any kind of therapeutic work it is important to get the consent of the person involved. Consent is important in confirming that the potential client understands what is involved and is willing to engage in whatever therapeutic relationship is offered.

The *Ethical Framework for Good Practice in Counselling and Psychotherapy* (Bond 2002), for example, refers to the notion of 'informed consent', implying that agreement has to be made based on the known facts involved. It is a meaningful factor in learning disabilities work as, historically, consent was not obtained for all kinds of practices and led to the abuse of people's rights. Obtaining consent is now seen as being necessary for any ethically based helping activity or treatment. Further ethical exploration on standards in talking therapy can be found in Tim Bond's *Standards and Ethics for Counselling in Action* (Bond 2000).

Contraindications (medication change)

Another factor which can impact on the effectiveness of therapeutic work is if clients are taking any medication, as this can affect the way that feelings are managed. It is important to be aware of medications that clients are taking prior to doing any therapeutic interventions.

Spoken and receptive language

The degree to which potential clients can process receptive language and also their ability to express themselves through speech and a degree of expressive language can affect the likelihood of success. For some individuals, including some with autism for example, there may be difficulties in communication which can impede the outcome of any therapy.

Language of client

Talking therapy relies on the dialogue being carried out in a language that is common to both therapist and client. Bereavement and loss work can highlight how important it is to express the feelings related to loss in a language that is accessible. Phrases and words in languages other than English can often capture the essence of a feeling or emotion and it is important that the concept involved is understood by both therapist and client.

Ability to sustain a therapeutic relationship

In assessing for therapeutic work, another key consideration is the ability of the potential client to sustain a therapeutic relationship over a period of time. For some clients the demands of therapy or counselling – being in a session with a therapist for up to an hour – can be emotionally, physically and psychologically demanding. As this relationship may be continued over a significant period of time, a potential client may need to be able to engage with a therapist for the duration or until the work comes to a conclusion.

History of attachments

A central part of the assessment in grief work, especially in the psychodynamic way of working, is the history of someone's attachments. This involves considering the way that attachments were formed and maintained from birth and any difficulties that there may have been. These can be strong indicators of future difficulties in grieving and mourning at times of bereavement, especially when a person's mother dies.

The early bond that is established between mother and child serves as a model for how subsequent relationships are and any disruption to this can set up difficulties in sustaining relationships. As many people with learning disabilities have difficult and traumatic birth experiences, this can be relevant to the way that therapeutic work is established.

Particular attention is paid to the following factors when assessing bereavement work and the likelihood of difficulties that may arise in subsequent work around relationships and transferences (i.e. who the therapist may come to represent): first, the strength of the attachment that the client had with the deceased person, and second, the nature of that attachment and how 'secure' it was.

Another relevant factor is any ambivalence or mixed feelings around the connection with the individual. This is particularly relevant if the grieving person felt that they were abandoned by their mother, for example.

The state of the relationship that was held at the time of death should be considered. If someone had a negative relationship with the person who died in the months prior to bereavement, this can be harder to resolve. For example, in a supported house where two individuals were in permanent conflict then, following the death of one, the surviving person can take longer to grieve following the loss.

Generally the greater the degree of dependency on the person who has died will be an indicator of more complex grief that is likely to present. The next section considers some of the factors that will form part of the assessment before any therapy begins.

Factors to consider in grief work

There is a recognition that individual and environmental circumstances can affect and disrupt the grief process. Researchers have referred to what happens when mourning cannot be completed, which is

> the intensification of grief to the level where the person is overwhelmed, resorts to maladaptive behaviour or remains interminably in the state of grief without of the mourning process towards completion…[it] involved processes that do not move progressively towards assimilation or accommodation but, instead, lead to stereotyped repetitions or extensive interruptions of healing. (Horowitz, Bonanno and Holen 1993)

Current situation of client

It is necessary to have a comprehensive overview of the current situation of the client concerned. This is usually given by the referrer, who is likely to be another professional who has knowledge of the client.

The living situation of someone is particularly relevant in terms of how well they may be able to make changes and whether it is a generally supportive environment or not.

Circumstances of grief

The most important consideration in assessing for bereavement work in learning disabilities is to find out whether or not the individual attended the funeral or not. This is seen as being a crucial indicator of subsequent work, because attending a funeral and having some kind of role or participation in it helps in the grief process by helping to accept the idea in more concrete terms. Not being able to attend funerals can be extremely hard for people, as it can set up fantasies about what actually happened.

Another consideration is how the individual found out about the death. It is possible that they were with the person at the time they died. However, hearing news from another source can be hard to believe especially if the informant is not known. In terms of understanding, being more informed or involved helps individuals with the grief process.

Is client's history known?

The amount of available history about referred clients can vary considerably. Some clients have long and well-documented histories that have been kept by social services and/or health teams for many years. Other referrals require a degree of information finding. Sometimes significant but previously unknown information can come up that explains how and why people present to talking therapy in the way that they do. Sometimes there is information on trauma or loss that can explain a whole forensic history and where therapeutic work has to be approached with caution and through work with mental health teams.

Accommodation history

Some bereaved clients have lived in the same accommodation for most of their lives. There is likely to be a significant difference between people who have moved a lot and had a disrupted history and people who lived in the same house with their family.

Past and present relationships

The quality of past and present relationships has a direct impact on what will be explored by clients in sessions. Picture cards and photographs or models may help to facilitate this and can give some perspective on an individual's experience. It is always important to know about any ruptures or difficulties in the relationships with the deceased person.

Previous separations and losses

It is important to get some idea of someone's previous experience of loss and separation as this gives an indication of how this was managed. Some clients will have had multiple losses and maybe found strategies to manage these, whereas others will not. In looking for current ways of managing loss, it is always helpful to think about what helped before.

View of the self

Having an indication of how someone sees their own identity and how people relate to others can be important when helping their current situation. Some people with learning disabilities do not have a clear view of how they come across to others; this can be because their view of themselves has not been promoted in the past. The result is that there can be poor self-concept which affects the way that change and adapting to loss takes place.

Resilience factors in place

In assessing for any talking therapy it is important to be able to identify what is currently in place that could act as a personal resource for someone facing grief. This involves looking at what qualities someone has that enables them to cope. It essentially involves looking to the past and present to assess what someone is already doing that helps them, and doing more of that.

Consulting those around the client as well as the client themselves about how they manage stress is another important factor.

Relationship with GP and other mental health professionals

If someone has a good existing relationship with their doctor and other professionals involved in their care, this is likely to be a good indicator for engagement in talking therapy. The therapeutic relationship is often said to rely on a good 'working alliance' between the therapist and the client.

General health

If someone's general health is not good, there is a risk of further deterioration following bereavement and other losses. The way that any talking therapy fits in to this will depend on the accessibility of the client and whether or not they think that talking to someone will help. For people with learning disabilities, the way that stress could affect their physical and psychological health has to be taken into consideration. Temporary decline in general health is common following bereavement, and having a learning disability could extend the length of time during which this occurs.

Memory and cognitive skills

It is important to have a sense of whether someone has the capacity to remember what has happened and link it to the way that they see themselves. Some people tend to 'rehearse' events that have happened and get stuck in their thinking around grief and loss. Doing this implies that there is room for change if there is the capacity to relate to others as well.

Support in between sessions

In a referral for bereavement work, it is important to think about what support someone has in place and about how change can be effected. Consider how previous changes and endings were managed. The context in which the client lives plays an important role here, including social, cultural and religious support that individuals and groups can offer. Having a shared belief system is part of this.

When there is minimal or no support, it may be that talking therapy becomes an essential focus for someone, or it can highlight the risks that someone faces of being on their own. Discussions with a referrer around existing support are essential to make sure that the client's emotional, physical and psychological needs are being met during the period of time that talking therapy takes place.

Unresolved grief

The complications that occur when people have not been able to work through their grief, either through not having the right support or by not having the capacity to make sense of what has happened, can lead to grief that is essentially unresolved and 'stuck'. The case study gives an illustration of this.

Case study: Andrew

'When we thought about when his behaviour change really started, we kept on going back to when his mum died. That's five years ago and he has never been the same since.' This quote came from a staff member who had worked at a residential service where Andrew had lived since his mum had become too frail to look after him. Following a heart attack, Andrew's mum had moved into a nursing home. The move had been sudden and Andrew went to respite care first, followed by a permanent move to residential care.

Following an initial period of settling in, Andrew got into a routine at the house and would visit his mum twice a week. He came back from each visit asking if they could 'both go back home' and was restless when he came back. After his mum's death 15 months later, he was understandably sad. A few months later he started to 'wander' and would occasionally go missing 'to go home', despite the fact that the nearby house had been sold about 18 months previously. Staff were concerned that he was going to get lost and arranged for him to do some new activities to 'keep his mind off the sad things'.

Although this helped initially, Andrew still kept searching for his old house. He knocked on the door of the house one day and the present owners answered. This was most distressing for Andrew, because he wanted to look around but he wasn't allowed in.

This reveals an unresolved grief that took a long time to move on and was eventually done by months of support both at his new home and through liaising with staff at the care centre to do some reminiscence work. Thinking wider than this, it is likely that some people never really resolve the issues surrounding bereavement and the loss it entails, especially if the relationship that is lost has been very close and interdependent.

Key points from this chapter

- Assessment remains a way of informing us of the relevant current and past factors that make up someone's reaction to grief.

- Having an informed view of someone's history enables us to work more effectively and create a stronger therapeutic alliance.

- Behavioural change is common following any loss or change and will always have a function. It is important not to jump to conclusions as the behaviour could be a temporary readjustment. Helping someone to maintain an emotionally safe home environment will help to lessen distress.

- It can be hard to notice some changes in behaviour that may pose risk although some are more obvious.

- If changes persist and are causing concern do get some help.

- Be alert over a longer period of time. Some grief reactions are likely to be delayed due to differing times for individuals to process information. The degree of learning disabilities and also individual situations will differ.

5

Developing Understanding around Bereavement and Loss

Context of the work

The extent to which clients were, historically, separated from family bereavements and losses in the past cannot be underestimated. It was as if, in society as a whole, the combination of disability and bereavement was viewed as being too much to bear. A historical legacy of the Victorian era was the separation of society's disabled from others.

Until the 1980s it was common for large Victorian institutions to be 'home' for a significant number of adults with learning disabilities, many of whom may have lived there for years. The population of these institutions was predominantly older, and some clients had lived there for 20 or more years. People with learning disabilities were shielded from grief and denied the equal right to participate in mourning. The focus of these institutions was around keeping people 'safe'. The exposure to many losses and risks was limited. With more opportunities to live a more independent life, there is greater exposure to loss but this has to be seen in the context of living a more 'normal' life.

Understanding what loss is about, and the implications that follow it, can be a complex process: we may understand the words that communicate death but not the changes that it will bring to our lives. We may have an idea of what the consequences will be following loss, but struggle to find a meaning for literally, spiritually or philosophically. This meaning can be located in our past – our personal histories – but becomes clear only in the light of experience.

Some people are still wary of speaking about death when around people with learning disabilities, as if it is a taboo subject, exposing them to an intolerable loss that they cannot help or contain and that they should be shielded from at all costs. At the same time, there has been a greater transparency around both disability and bereavement in recent times that has led to a greater awareness of the issues that people with learning disabilities, and those who care for them, face.

Although still variable in terms of their psychological centredness, services have become less remote and there has been a diminishing of the shame that has previously been associated at some level with the experience of this client group. Although learning disability services in the UK have had major reviews on both national and government levels, access to specific bereavement services has not been pushed up the agenda in the same way that other more visible areas of social policy have.

Recent scandals of health care in the UK have highlighted failings in the health care needs for people with learning disabilities. Making services accessible across the board of physical and mental health needs is something that we all need to be mindful and watchful of.

Perhaps the most valuable thing that we can offer to people with disabilities who are facing loss, or trying to make sense of the changes that bereavement brings, is acceptance and a willingness to put time aside when communication and understanding are a problem. This also touches upon deeper questions about what loss tells us about the human condition and how it is manifest in behaviour, beliefs and relationships.

Facing loss, whether through illness or disability, can be the start of a process of reflection for those involved where change and acceptance begin to happen.

Practical considerations

It is now considered good practice and in the best interests of the client wherever possible to provide reasons why their relative or friend has died. Whether there is an initial understanding of this or not, avoiding telling someone about a bereavement can make it more difficult to introduce it at a later stage. Fantasies can be set up or amplified about what has happened to the deceased person, making it harder for the individual to be involved and leading to exclusion.

It is not uncommon for different groups of people connected to an individual to have conflicting opinions about how bereavement is introduced and managed. A key consideration has to be a client's existing knowledge of the situation. Work can be done to prepare clients for a future loss that can be referred back to when it is likely that a death is imminent. This can be extremely important and empowering for those expecting a loss and can involve discussion around health, illness and ageing as well as being open with others about what is possible in terms of support and care.

The change of routine and weekly contacts that bereavement can bring is likely to cause a great deal of fear, anticipation and instability. The fear of a future loss, such as when an elderly parent will die, can build up to be a huge dread, but talking with someone about their fears and of how they imagine that they will cope can help someone to feel reassured if approached in the right way. This work should be done in an appropriate setting – one to one, or in a small group discussion or review meeting – but talking about fears can help to diminish them.

Blocks to understanding

A significant challenge facing people with learning disabilities is when there are blocks to understanding. We can often assume that the problem with this is located in the individual who has the learning disability. However, it is more helpful to think about our own role, as a society and as individuals in the construction of these blocks. Communication is such a broad and dynamic sphere that there are ways of adapting to meet the needs of individuals concerned and to think about how we manage our own understanding of loss.

The following examples are often part of the problem.

Conveying information ambiguously

Explaining or talking about death is never easy, especially if you are the person who has to convey the news. For that moment you know that you have something to say which is likely to upset someone and could well be upsetting to you too. It may show in your face or in your body language, and this may further distress the person you are telling. The greatest risk is that what you actually say is not clear and has the chance of being misinterpreted. Keeping language clear and unambiguous is essential, especially if the individual concerned cannot hold attention for long.

Communicating too bluntly or too vaguely

Communicating news of loss or death is never an easy task. It can be even more difficult explaining it to people with learning disabilities, as we can be very aware of the responsibilities involved in looking after their emotional and practical well-being. It is often hard to know what to say and how to say it. However, knowing someone well can enable you to know the best way to approach the subject and anticipating how they are likely to react and their trust in you will also help.

Giving the news in the wrong place

The environment in which news of a death or major change in a relative's condition is conveyed is very important. If the setting is wrong then the impact can be profound. There are cases where the most sensitive news has been communicated in a public place that has been totally inappropriate. Things have improved in recent years in hospitals and homes. News is usually shared in a private, if impersonal, space that reflects the nature of what is being said and respects the dignity of those involved.

Often news comes to people who live in a residential setting via the manager or senior staff on duty. Most places have protocols for these situations.

Using euphemisms misleadingly

Accurate language should be used – such as died or dead – rather than euphemisms that are used with good intent to cushion the blow, as these could lead to confusion. The words and terms used should be based on what has actually happened rather than terms such as 'gone to heaven' or 'sleeping with the angels' or even 'they are with God now'. Of course some people will still prefer to use euphemisms, but it has to be recognized for many people with learning disabilities who have a more literal understanding of language that being told different things by different people can create confusion and distress.

Communicating inadequately

Not being able to communicate and be understood can further complicate the process of grief. The person conveying the news may have been upset themselves, which can be difficult. Or, as described in the stages of grief, shock and disbelief can prevent us from taking in or registering news of death.

In our own distraction through grief, sometimes the explanation of what happened and why can affect understanding too. We may assume that the person we are explaining to understands the implication of what we are saying and what it means, but that is not guaranteed.

Building on previous understanding

Building on previous knowledge and understanding can help with managing current loss and grief. Exposure to loss and grief can give people resources with which to face a similar situation. Although many people with learning disabilities have experienced many subliminal losses, these may not have been recognized so cannot be accessed easily.

In her book *Loss and Learning Disability*, Noelle Blackman (2003) points to the importance of a number of contextual and cognitive factors that can make the loss process easier: 'The balance between cognitive understanding, life experience and the quality of support offered at the time of bereavement are still crucial factors' (Blackman 2003, p.38). Blackman also notes that there is less material on bereavement and people with learning disabilities than there is on bereavement in childhood.

Questions that can help both individuals and staff supporting them are the following:

- What other losses, however small, has the person faced?
- How did they manage this and adapt to the change that it brought?
- What did we put in place to make it easier for that individual?

Looking to past losses and the way that they were managed can be valuable resources to have in managing current situations. Other key questions arising from this for staff and carers can include:

- What made change easier to cope with last time?
- Who would be the best or most comfortable people to support the person in facing this change?
- What are the benefits that could come from this change or loss in the longer term?

It is not uncommon for people with learning disabilities to know other people who have coped with major loss and life change. On a practical level there is some thinking that can be done around how these other people managed and how that may be applied to the individual concerned. This is a kind of 'death education' that comes from observing other people and the situations that others face.

Autism and understanding of bereavement and loss

If you are caring for someone with an autistic diagnosis who is facing bereavement or loss, this can require specific thinking and planning. Autism is a developmental disability that affects someone's emotional, social and mental development. It was first identified in 1943 by Leo Kanner, who drew attention to the fact that there were nine key factors that played a part in autism. The most relevant of these are: delayed speech and language development; a presenting detachment from others in communication and relationships leading to a lack of reciprocal communication, and a desire for activities and routines to remain the same (i.e. not coping well with change). Kanner identified this group as having similar behaviours and this led to the term 'autistic' or 'autism'. The word 'autism' comes from the Greek word 'autos' meaning 'self'.

Autism is characterized by difficulties in behaving and thinking in a flexible way, difficulties in interacting and interpreting social interaction and in communication with others. It is common for people with autism to repeat phrases that are said to them as if wanting to make sense of them but for the more subtle meanings to be overlooked.

The negotiation around social relationships and communicating with others means that adapting to any new situations can be extremely hard for some. Spiller and Gratsa (2004) state that autism can change over time but that a degree of support is likely to be needed during adulthood.

A significant number of people with an autism diagnosis also have a learning disability. For these clients, bereavement and loss can pose some problems in anticipating change, understanding death especially if it has occurred from a distance and also understanding the wider concepts of bereavement.

As autism can affect the way that people interact socially – affecting their interpersonal relationships – this can present as a further difficulty at occasions associated with death, such as funerals. It is often hard to present the process of death and loss in a logical way, particularly if facts and emotions become confused.

It is possible to familiarize clients with bereavement if they have experienced it before and if it was well managed. As with everything a good and trusting relationship with the bereaved client can be the most helpful aspect of managing bereavements.

It is often common for clients who have autism to experience the whole area of bereavement in a detached way. Their response can be to express their loss and stress by an increase in ritualistic behaviours.

Communication

Having autism can complicate one's fluency and confidence in speaking. This is likely to be because of the difficulties in communication and taking in information that is being said. For people who have difficulties in conveying and receiving information, it can be very hard to understand loss and its impact. There is often a problem in understanding the meaning and implication of what is said and, following on from that, making sense of what is said. This will be relevant to the understanding of change that comes from a loss.

Some people who are on the autistic spectrum do not communicate easily through everyday conversation and, following loss or news of change, may become withdrawn as if trying to take in what they have heard. Some clients who have elements of echolalia may become more so following news of loss as a response to the anxiety and uncertainty that they feel.

The absence of emotional affect following such news can make it hard to assess the impact of a loss but observing and being sensitive to behavioural change in the weeks and months after can give an indication of how someone is coping.

Social interaction

Following a loss it may be difficult for people with autistic spectrum disorders to communicate their feelings in the same way as others. They may not know how to respond following a bereavement. Occasions such as funerals and memorial services can be anxiety provoking for some people with autism for example. Repetitive behaviours may inhibit social relationships and losing someone who was the only person who you thought understood you can lead to further isolation and social anxiety.

Rigid thinking

Rigid or inflexible thinking can be an extra barrier to understanding for many people with autistic spectrum disorders, for example in not being able to accept change in routine when facing loss of home or death of a friend. Many people with autism and Asperger syndrome find it hard to adjust their thinking. Bereavements and losses are hard for any of us to get used to when they happen but with conditions that result in people having more rigid thinking, this can affect the ability to think about wider meaning and where people 'go' after death. Abstract explanations which sometimes try to make explaining loss 'kinder' can often result in greater confusion when there is rigid thinking; it is also harder for people in this position to use their imagination.

In short, rigid thinking can provide unambiguous answers but can trap people. The language used in explaining change is often less certain and ends with frustration when clients ask why losses happen. Often there are no clear answers and exposure to several bereavements can become part of the fixed stories that people use to explain death that are not helpful.

Developing an understanding of illness

People with learning disabilities, particularly those over the age of 40, will have had a number of mixed messages about health and illness: in childhood they may have been subjected to a whole range of invasive procedures in hospital, especially if there has been an identified neurological cause of their disability. If there was a learning disability suspected, the attitude of family and professionals may have changed as more evidence was gathered of neurological damage that could have a lasting impact.

Depending on the severity of the disability, the geographical availability of services (which were frequently minimal locally) and the attitude of their families, many clients would at some point have faced the prospect or the reality of living in an institution or large care home where individual rights were not respected and standards of care were variable. Frequently these would be in isolated locations where the large hospitals developed their own sense of community.

In considering how people could develop an understanding of illness, several important factors have to be considered: first, the individual's relationship to themselves and their bodies, second, the ability to articulate change or pain, and third, the availability of services that could identify symptoms and understand differing levels of communication.

Illnesses can change an individual's lifestyle and create unwelcome limits on what one can do. In learning disabilities the potential consequences of illness are not always noticed, explained or understood. There is also a loss of power that is associated with illnesses. The role of health education and improvements in access to health screening has enabled a much more proactive stance in this.

Developing an understanding of what death is

Some people with learning disabilities find it difficult to make sense of things in abstract or symbolic terms. This is often associated with autism, where changes are hard to adapt to and events are taken quite literally. Making sense of what happens seems to be something that is urgently needed but hard to do for such clients. There can be a real confusion between 'death', 'temporary separation' and when people are just not around for a set period of time.

It can be hard to come up with an explanation for why someone dies or why change is necessary. If you feel under stress yourself as a carer, you may not be able to explain what has happened in a way that is possible to grasp. It is also important to try to be consistent at a time when people want clear unambiguous answers. If someone's death has been comparatively sudden and with little or no warning, this can add to the feeling that it is a bit surreal or not believable.

Breaking news of sudden illness or death in residential settings

Explanations of the reason for any changes are often fraught with further problems, if one person in a residential home moves away suddenly due to illness or hospital admission, or if they die.

Sadly in some settings death and illness are common occurrences and both staff and clients may become resigned to what may seem an inevitable part of living and working there. This should not be taken for granted, as it can ultimately lead to risks of an impersonal type of care.

Staff support, team meetings and training strategies should reflect the potential impact that this can have on staff and other long-term clients. In situations like this it is worth bearing in mind the following suggestions:

- Whenever possible prepare for any changes. If someone you care for is facing a period of change, try to introduce the change and give a reason for that change. Encourage the person involved to talk about it and answer questions as unambiguously as possible.

- Keep to a familiar routine as far as possible so that there is no unnecessary additional disruption. Inform any day centre or club that the person attends so that they can be aware of why the person may be upset or distressed.

- Don't force the other residents to go to activities in the evening, but if they want to then encourage them to go.

- If someone lives in a shared house with others and one resident is admitted to hospital, reassure the other residents, but do not give certainties about their condition such as 'They will be home soon' or 'They are bound to get better – there is nothing to worry about.' Such explanations may give the person relief in the short term but can be seen as a massive betrayal of trust if the person concerned deteriorates and has to move elsewhere or dies.

- Focus on being realistic, e.g. 'They are not well at the moment and we all hope that they feel more comfortable soon.'

- If it is clear that the person involved is not going to get better, it is important to state this. Check out what ideas are held by others about the hospitalized resident so that their thoughts are voiced rather than turning into fantasies and fears about what has happened. Such fears could easily be distorted when they think about their own future.

- Reassure wherever possible and say that the hospitalized resident is being well looked after. Encourage the worried housemate to visit with someone if this is possible and if they want to. Otherwise they could write to the hospitalized resident or send some flowers as a way of keeping them in their thoughts.

These points are relevant to anyone we work with. However, it is important to consider how other people who know the ill or recently deceased person will react. Most homes will have a wider network of people who come and visit regularly. Knowing how others are likely to react based on their existing relationships can help to support them if necessary when these situations occur.

Reading social cues

Some people with learning disabilities are unable to read social clues accurately. This can be particularly hard when faced with a situation when there is a lot of grief or distress around following a bereavement.

The questions 'How should we react or look or behave when people are crying?' or 'How should I behave when we are at a funeral?' often come up at this point. 'How or what should I feel?' is another unexpressed question for many people. Of course there is no 'should' involved but some clients do not know how to react following bereavement.

Sometimes people appear detached as if it has not registered or they are not concerned, and this may well be the case. Other clients may express their grief by crying very loudly in a way that others may feel is inappropriate outside of an immediate family member or close friend. Others may just be confused by what has happened and how to respond. These questions often lend themselves to therapeutic work in counselling or psychotherapy (see Chapter 6).

Although there may be some basic social rules about what not to do, people do respond in different ways to death, loss and change.

Different attachments in residential care

Some people in residential care will have known each other and lived together for many years. Many of these relationships may predate the staff who work there currently or predate the history of the shared home that they live in. Many clients may have known each other for 30 years from institutionalized care in a hospital setting.

It is important to recognize that these relationships will have been witness to a shared history. Being separated from someone with a shared history of this sort can have a profound and often unspoken impact. It can tap into other fears that are discussed below.

Difficulty in locating the body

Sometimes it can be hard to believe that someone has died when we have not seen them for a while. It is common for people with learning disabilities to base their experiences on certainties and the day-to-day interaction with others. It may be easier to believe that someone has died if you knew that they were ill or if you saw them become ill in front of you. Particularly for people on the autistic spectrum, it is easier to believe and see in concrete terms. When circumstances change suddenly, it can be hard to conceptualize what might have happened and there can be a desire for certainty that is not possible to gain.

Seeking certainty is an inevitable consequence of 'not knowing' and this can be very hard for some people to settle or to be 'at peace' with following a bereavement or change. Questions remain about the meaning of what has happened and the reason for it.

Questions and assumptions may be made about 'what happens next' in terms of where people 'go' after death. If someone has a particular faith or belief then this can be easier to explain and understand (e.g. 'They are with Allah' or 'They have gone to heaven'). Other people worry about where someone has gone and it is best to work with their beliefs rather than try to impose your own.

Explaining change to people with learning disabilities

Other major changes other than bereavement have to be considered and deserve explanation when working with this client group, for example when other clients or staff leave a service, or when clients or staff die.

When other clients leave a residential or day service

When someone leaves a residential service (for a different service, for hospice care or for another reason) it can be very unsettling for other people within that service. Often they will have had a shared history and there is often a sense of loss and concern if someone 'moves on', even if the person has not died. In this situation it is essential to provide some explanation to others in a house as to why someone is leaving. If there is time, it is helpful for other people to say goodbye or have some farewell event to mark the change. If someone has had to leave a home following a sudden health crisis, it is important to let others who are still at the house take part in saying goodbye, so that they take some ownership over what has happened.

When staff leave

When permanent staff leave day and residential services, they take with them special attachments that have built up over months and years. Key working relationships are often particularly significant as they require that clients have a greater sense of identity and trust with the staff involved. Feelings of insecurity can sometimes follow someone leaving, because the change is outside of the client's control.

In this situation the following points are useful if you are leaving a service:

- Be honest and clear about leaving and state what date you are leaving.

- Don't feel pressured to give a detailed explanation as to why you are leaving, but some explanation does help.

- Be clear about leaving and don't promise to come back if you know that you cannot do so or say that you are likely to see people out and about in the area if you are not.

- If you are leaving and you have some bad feelings towards the service management or other staff, try not to say this around clients as it is inviting them to side with you or the other people involved, which is not fair on them.

- If you have to leave suddenly, try to write a letter to the people you were caring for explaining that you are leaving and cannot come back, as this lessens the risk that clients will think that it is something that they have done that is to blame.

When clients die

Sadly, clients die and this can have a big impact on the staff caring for them and the other people who are at the day or residential service or college. This can take time to get used to, especially if the deceased person has been part of the service for some years. Other clients attending the same day or residential service should be told honestly about it and given the opportunity, where possible, to attend the funeral of the deceased person.

Even though we know that there is a statistically higher chance that people with learning disabilities may have particular long-term health conditions and will die, it can still be a shock and a reminder of the vulnerability of many of the people who we work with.

When staff die

Sometimes staff working with people with learning disabilities will die. This can be particularly upsetting for both staff and clients and can be more unexpected, because events like this are not 'supposed' to happen. In situations like this it is important to be honest with clients and give some kind of explanation or reason. Talking with clients about this is hard to do but is a necessary part of everyone feeling included and sharing in part of the experience. It also avoids clients building up fantasies about what might have happened.

Holding a short memorial service which clients can create themselves can give voice to the thoughts around the loss of staff and other clients who were known and have died. This can be some time after the death and can be healing, especially if people were not able to attend a funeral.

Health education and awareness

It is necessary to have an understanding of illness and the different factors that contribute to it in order to make sense of it. Explaining facts about health and why the body reacts as it does to changes in it has been something that has been avoided historically. People with learning disabilities have been shielded from the realities of illness by the belief that 'they would not understand'. They can also have negative beliefs about their presentation and bodies that can impact on health.

Thankfully this has begun to change. Health policy for people with learning disabilities as well as for the general population through the National Service Frameworks has encouraged a greater awareness of health needs. A more integrated approach to health care needs is helping people with learning disabilities to avoid being isolated.

In his book on health psychology, Edward Sarafino (1998) proposes that illnesses are triggered and affected by combinations of biological, psychological and social factors. The development of the 'bio-psychosocial' approach to understanding illness has helped people to have a more integrated understanding of the different factors affecting individuals and through looking at these has enabled people to take greater control over their general health. Previous to this the biomedical model was more concerned with 'deviation from the norm'.

Being aware of the interaction of these factors can not only be preventative but also help individuals to take a greater role in the course of their illness. While not creating a cure, the bio-psychosocial model can help individuals to improve their general health. The three areas and the relevance to learning disability are the biological (focusing on the cause of the illness and how it effects the body), the psychological (dealing with the way that behaviour, thoughts and emotions play a role in defining the way that illness is managed by an individual) and the social or interpersonal (concerning the social and interpersonal relationships and support that the person has).

Specific illness

In terms of how illness is managed, the relationship with health and social care professionals has to be thought about and nurtured carefully. Having a named nurse to be a liaison between hospital and the patient concerned can be helpful in reducing misinformation and being a trusted but neutral person to guide someone through the course of their illness and treatment. This is a role that has become increasingly relevant to older clients who live independently but whose main carers are either deceased or unable to facilitate this role.

Case study: James

James was 58 when he developed a form of diabetes that was resistant to improvement through diet alone. He had previously lived with his mum, but she had died when he was 50 and he then went to live in a supported tenancy flat with other people. Since his mum's death, James had struggled to maintain a balanced diet and would be tempted to eat what he wanted. Living more independently, he resisted the advice and interventions of support staff and would eat what he wanted for most of the time, which over a period of time triggered diabetes. It was recognized that he was a bit of a 'comfort eater' and that his low mood was stopping him from making dietary changes and keeping to them.

At this stage a learning disabilities community nurse specialist became involved in James's care and began to put some firm boundaries around what he could and could not eat. The nurse explained why things had to be balanced in terms of diet and the importance of exercise. The relationship was a focus for his progress, however, and building up trust relied on him thinking it was worth changing.

Constructing a programme that was clear and gave him some choices helped James to begin to follow the programme, which began to moderate and stabilize the condition. The main focus was on building his understanding of illness and changes in the body that result from eating the wrong type of food. As his belief was that he could eat whatever he liked 'while no one was looking', it took some time to build trust, change his behaviour so that he was doing this 'for him' rather than for anyone else.

Impact of a death within a shared supported house

At some stage, maybe triggered by a serious illness or declining health, a decision is made by parents or carers of people living 'at home' that a move to some kind of residential or supportive housing is necessary for the person they have been looking after. Many parents are realistic about this and have put plans in place, preparing for any such move by encouraging their son or daughter to have overnight stays at a supported house as 'respite'. Ideally a more permanent move to the designated house should be planned so that when the parent or carer does eventually die the surviving person with learning disabilities is already in a familiar setting.

Having staff in place who have an awareness of bereavement and the issues it brings is important at such times but can be difficult if there are unexpected losses that occur in a relatively short space of time.

Case study: Richard

Richard lived in a staffed house for three men. He had moved into the house a few months before his mother died. She had talked with him about her illness, that she was not going to get better, and that it was best for him to move so that he could settle into a new home and 'get to know some new friends'. Richard did not have any brothers and sisters. A place had become available at a local house and so he moved in.

Generally the transition from living with his mum to the staffed house went well and when his mum died four months later, he commented that it was good that he had moved because it would have been upsetting 'if she had died while he was in the house'. He was well supported leading up to, during and after the bereavement.

Two months later one of the other residents died suddenly and unexpectedly. He had had no major signs of illness and, despite being in his early seventies, his death was a shock to everyone as he had a good medical history. Richard attended the funeral at his own choice with staff and the other resident from the house.

A month or so later a new man moved into the house. Richard was keen to help him to settle in; he already knew him from the local

Gateway club. Richard felt that he was helping, which also reduced his anxiety about being seen as the new person in the house. It helped him to feel more secure in himself and he enjoyed feeling that he had some kind of role.

During the autumn, five months later, the other original member of the house had a heart attack and died suddenly. Although Richard wasn't as close to him as the other resident who had died, this sudden death shocked him. In the past three months a number of established staff had left and had been replaced by agency staff who, although caring, did not know Richard from when he moved into the house.

Richard was referred for some counselling sessions as it was felt that he would benefit from 'talking to someone from outside'. In sessions he presented as being very quiet, as if he was stunned into silence by a number of repeated losses. After another, younger man moved into the house, he said how he worried that he would be 'next to go', because the other two people he knew when he moved in had died within a short time.

Avoiding euphemisms

When faced with explaining a death, many people who are around people with learning disabilities are tempted to avoid the actuality of what has happened. They may avoid using the words 'death', 'died' and 'dying', being fearful that it may be psychologically damaging for people. In a bid to limit the upset caused to those affected, some people still think it is kinder to use different language and euphemisms. Quite often this can be more about our own fears around death or the discomfort about explaining something that we know will upset the person who is concerned.

Phrases such as 'She has passed away', 'She has gone to heaven' or 'She has gone to a better place' can not only be misleading but also complicate the understanding of the person concerned. As practitioners working with people who have learning disabilities, especially with people who have quite concrete thinking, it is important that our language is not confusing and conveys the information needed in a clear and unambiguous way.

If people we are caring for subsequently talk about what has happened in an ambiguous way and it seems that they may have misunderstood, it is important to recheck their understanding. Sometimes this may feel a bit blunt, but it clarifies the situation for the person concerned.

Thinking about funerals and attending funerals

Thinking about the practicalities concerning attending funerals is vital to ensure that this central part of the grief process is managed as well as possible. It is essential that people with learning disabilities have the same opportunities to attend the funeral of people that they love, namely those in family relationships and significant relationships to them. Being at a funeral, however distressing it may appear to be for everyone concerned, gives individuals the chance to participate in their grief with others. The support of others can be seen at the time of the funeral and the act of being with others to mourn has a reparative function.

A significant minority of people with learning disabilities do not attend their parents' funerals. A study by Hollins and Esterhuyzen (1997) estimated that the figure was about 54 per cent. Although this may have improved over the last few years, this is still a notable percentage who either cannot or do not attend. The reasons for this may be complex but the overriding suggestion is that people with learning disabilities are not encouraged to take an active role in saying goodbye. It may be easier to hide away rather than face the loss of someone close.

Attending a funeral is an important part of saying farewell to someone. However, the extent of involvement that families have can vary across faiths and cultures. Confusion and distress can occur during a cremation or burial. Cremations for example can be confusing for people with learning disabilities because the body is left behind in the crematorium as mourners walk away. Burials are also confusing for some people but there is a greater sense of what is happening to the body and the finality of leaving it in the ground.

If possible it is advisable to talk through what happens before the service, otherwise people can feel very confused about where the body goes. At this point explanations can become rather abstract and many people, especially those who process information more literally, can still be asking 'What happens to him/her now?' People may experience guilt around leaving the scene of the cremation or burial as they may feel that they should not have done so.

Some individuals voice their questions or anxieties about what is happening at the funeral service itself; it can feel very poignant that they have not understood, adding to their distress. Preparing people for what is likely to happen before the service itself can reduce the likelihood of this.

Guidance for family members and staff

As this is an important area to consider the following points offer guidance for other family members or staff:

- People with learning disabilities have the right to attend funeral services of family and close friends and should be supported if they wish to go, as it is an integral part of the grieving process. However, if they clearly do not wish to attend, then they should not be made to.

- Do some preparatory thinking about how you can support someone at a funeral. If you are going with a small group of someone's friends then discuss what will happen at the service. It is usually possible to contact those holding the service beforehand. Some thinking could be done about the way that people attend as groups.

- Think ahead about what sort of ceremony it is likely to be so that it is not a surprise. Access should be thought about for wheelchair users including if there is a burial that requires going to a graveside.

- If people wish to give flowers, they should be supported to do so. Again this involves thinking ahead.

The above points are important in enabling people with learning disabilities to take as great a part in mourning as they wish to. After the burial it is important to think about what happens next in terms of being with family members and how that is best facilitated.

Finding it hard to move on from worry

If someone has had recent experience of a bereavement or loss, it can be easy to 'catastrophize' or confuse what can happen from one experience to another. This can be part of rigid thinking as well, assuming that one person's experience will automatically happen to others.

Case study: Jenny

Jenny had lived with her long-term carer, Annie, for over 12 years. Jenny had moved there following the unexpected death of her mum and was known to have found change to be difficult. Sadly her mum had died suddenly in hospital following complications during a routine operation. As it was unexpected, there had to be an autopsy, which took some time to arrange due to administrative and technical difficulties at the hospital.

This left Jenny with several anxieties and made her transition to her new carer more difficult. For about a week she had no clear answer about what had happened and could not see her mum's body 'to say goodbye'. Afterwards in a review meeting it was agreed that this had been unhelpful but inevitable. Although she did say goodbye to her mum, she needed a lot of reassurance around where her mum's body had been and why the funeral was later than people originally said it was going to be.

When Annie died, suddenly and unexpectedly, Jenny was at the day centre that she attended. Annie had recently had surgery to her leg and there was concern that there had been post-operative infection that had turned gangrenous and may require partial amputation. Jenny was aware that Annie had had problems with her leg and had overheard one of the centre workers talking about how these things 'can turn nasty'.

When Jenny heard that Annie had died she began to ask about Annie's leg and if that was what had 'made her die'. She went to respite care for about a week following this and was reassured by social workers that Annie had died of natural causes and not because of her bad leg.

After attending Annie's funeral, however, Jenny became very distressed and began to question what had happened to her. Unlike her mum, she had not seen Annie's body. Having only seen the coffin when she went into the church, she asked where Annie's body was and if her leg had been taken off because it was 'bad for her'. Carers who were with her tried to reassure her but she became worried particularly after the funeral.

Talking about it months later Jenny said to her key worker that she was worried about what had happened to Annie. Jenny had started to get some muscular pain in her leg and started to panic that she was 'going to die' or have her leg 'taken off'. She was referred to a nurse when her symptoms continued and then Jenny told her that she remembered how 'legs can turn nasty and you die with that and then you are in a coffin'. A referral was then made to a psychologist who identified that Jenny's fears were based on what had happened.

Helping someone to move on from worry
Jenny's case study illustrates the following points:

- Clear explanations are crucial.

- Any doubts are to be answered as honestly as possible.

- Some people see things very literally; placement of the body and integrity of the body are important.

- A person's sense of loss can be managed better if there is some understanding.

- People do move on but badly managed transitions will reinforce damaged attachments and loss.

Growing older

For some people with learning disabilities, the experience of bereavement or having a serious illness can raise existential questions around their own identity. Having a disability can also raise these questions and at times these areas present with individuals as either depression or loss around life. Often people keep these worries to themselves. It is important to be aware of behavioural changes or conversations that may indicate these questions.

People with learning disabilities are likely to have witnessed other people that they know who have died early or have experienced chronic illness leading to questions such as 'Why has this loss happened to me?', 'Where is my life going?', 'Who or what am I in terms of other people who know me?' These kind of questions can resurface at times of change and transition; although they may not be articulated by people we work with, they will still be part of psychological change and questioning.

Key points from this chapter

- Understanding is the most important factor in resolving distress around bereavement and loss. Grief is a normal response to life events such as this.

- Focusing on communication and the means of explaining loss to clients can facilitate an easier process.

- Working with what is already known is a good way to increase knowledge around bereavement and loss and takes away some of the unexpected when it happens.

6

Therapeutic Tasks

Introduction

This chapter focuses on the tasks found in therapeutic relationships in talking therapy with clients. Much of this will come from the observations and practice of bereavement work with learning disabled clients in psychotherapy and counselling interventions but can also be applied to other relationships where there is longer-term contact with clients following loss and bereavement work.

Most professional relationships with people with learning disabilities will involve a therapeutic element. From the first contact with someone, dependency is established quickly. Trust is important as well as the need for consistency. Many professional relationships last for some months or even years and can take on an important role in clients' lives.

There has been much written about what counselling and psychotherapy are as well as what the nature of a good 'therapeutic relationship' involves. In the context of learning disabilities there are a number of factors to consider that make approaching the work different. These will work across professions and so will have relevance.

Types of referrals

It is common for referrals to professionals to be made in different ways to anticipate and manage loss. There is no right time necessarily to make a referral but types of referrals include preventative referrals, immediate referrals, complex systemic referrals and delayed referrals.

Preventative referrals

Some referrals are initiated when someone is going to be facing a bereavement or major change in the short to medium term. Having somewhere to talk about anticipated change can be helpful and can also alleviate the concerns that support staff and workers can have about future loss and separation. One drawback to this, however, is that it can be hard to find a focus and can also raise alarm in the referred client.

Immediate referrals

There is often a concern that straight after a bereavement, a client needs immediate counselling sessions to talk about what has happened. Although this can be what is required, it is often better to wait until a situation has settled. Sessions immediately after a bereavement can add to the client's perception of disorientation as they are out of routine and can evoke confusion in individuals. Bereavement is nearly always followed by a funeral; counselling or therapy sessions would not usually begin until the necessary ceremonies have taken place.

Complex systemic referrals

Bereavement can often involve systemic aspects as they affect the wider network around a client. Sometimes following a bereavement issues of guardianship and responsibility arise within families around a client. Systemic or family therapy referrals can follow this and can be helpful in addressing outstanding issues.

Delayed referrals

Sometimes following bereavement there can be a kind of inertia about the best way to support someone. This can result in delayed referral where the presenting bereavement, loss or change has happened a long time ago and where the immediacy of it has gone. It can feel as if what would have been helpful at one point has now passed and the situation has changed. At this point there may be some disadvantages in starting sessions as it is likely to bring back grief when the individual is coping well enough and it is counterproductive to begin sessions.

Establishing a good therapeutic relationship

In establishing a therapeutic relationship it is essential to ensure that the mode of working and the way in which the work takes place enable the physical and psychological safety of both the counsellor and the client. The following areas are essential to consider before any therapeutic work begins.

Consent

Most clients who are referred to any therapeutic intervention following bereavement come to address the impact of the loss they have experienced. It could be that they have requested this themselves, but it is more likely that other professionals who are involved in their care will have made the referral.

At this point, consent becomes an important issue. Entering any kind of therapeutic relationship requires the consent of the individual involved. The UK Department of Health (2001a) publication, *Consent: A Guide for People with Learning Disabilities* states that giving consent to any intervention should require that the individual is competent at taking decisions, is acting voluntarily and is provided with sufficient information to make a decision. Consent is seen as being a process rather than a one-off decision which takes into account the person's understanding of the benefits and risks of going ahead with whatever intervention they are offered.

In assessing whether therapeutic work is appropriate, it is essential in talking therapy to check if clients are understanding what is being talked about. Consent should be checked prior to a referral and also at the start of a piece of work.

Contract

In working with any client referred for counselling, the contract is central to the therapeutic process in that it establishes the terms and conditions within which the therapist and the client will work together. There is likely to be a difference in learning disabilities work as the contract may involve the implicit involvement of other people to facilitate it. Understanding the contract may be complex to some people and the agreement may be different from other agreements that the client will have established with other professionals. There are likely to be clauses built into a contract so that help can be sought if necessary.

Most of all, having an agreed contract is important in loss and bereavement work so that clients will not 'lose' the therapist without warning. In this sense it mirrors good endings in any relationships with people who have limited power in being able to effect change: this ending can be different as there is a negotiation around when the therapeutic relationship ends.

Confidentiality

Confidentiality is integral to successful therapeutic work and potentially works on many levels. A certain amount of information may already be known to services and have confidentiality clauses around it. The sharing of information on a client's behalf can be complex to negotiate and to work within. As well as keeping information safe, confidentiality extends to the keeping of written records. In the UK the law has made this clear with the Data Protection Act 1998 setting out clear guidelines around what information can be shared.

In their book *The Values of Psychotherapy*, Jeremy Holmes and Richard Lindley (1989) talk about how psychotherapy and counselling work 'includes fantasies and fears and feelings which patients find very hard to acknowledge, even to themselves... This feeling of safety requires a strong understanding that what happens in therapy be strictly between therapist and client' (Holmes and Lindley 1989).

In learning disabilities, different expectations apply around confidentiality. If material emerges that concerns the current physical or psychological safety, then measures need to be put in place to ensure that the individual is not at risk. Sometimes in the therapeutic relationship 'secrets' may be shared that are important to keep safe; clients should be able to talk about their histories to give their past a voice. Telling someone a secret means that there is an implicit trust that the person hearing it will treat this responsibly.

Boundary setting

The boundaries that are established in the therapeutic work are at the core of bereavement work if you are an outside professional. Maintaining appropriate boundaries in family relationships is also important in learning disabilities work. Boundaries relate to what is going to be talked about in a safe way, to the time and place of sessions, what will be shared with others (such as carers), and what needs to remain confidential. By making the work safe it is possible for clients to have a different experience of talking to someone who is impartial and separate from the rest of their lives, but who is trained to be able to hold difficult information, and to process and manage the transferential aspects of the relationship. This enables clients to be able to work through difficult feelings and bad experiences.

Many people with learning disabilities find it more difficult to differentiate between the boundaries between themselves and others than between themselves and the wider world. Finding ways of interacting with the world in a meaningful way is a complex task for anyone, particularly following the prolonged loss that a bereavement can bring. Establishing consistent boundaries in a therapeutically based relationship can give a different sense of continuity and prepare for a different type of ending, where instead of being 'left' by others, they can leave themselves on different terms.

Environment and room setting

The environment in which therapeutic work takes place is important in providing safety and neutrality. Safety should extend to physical as well as psychological considerations. It is important to consider how a room is set out, for example that the chairs are of similar height and that there are no noise distractions. It is also important not to obstruct the door. If doing any kind of talking therapy in a day service, it is advisable to check that there is an appropriate room in which to meet with the client and that other people know that you are doing the work at the stated time.

Goal setting

It is common when doing therapeutic work for some goals to be set either directly with the client or that a practitioner can identify as being relevant to a client's progress. Worden (2003, p.52) identifies some common goals of grief counselling as follows:

- First, to increase the reality of a loss that has been experienced. This is to enable the client to begin to adjust to the situation as it actually is and to move away from any idea that it has not really happened. In facing the reality of a loss, the work of starting to manage it can begin.

- Second, to help the client to begin to manage feelings that are being expressed and those that are hidden. Doing this in a way that respects the client's process is very important as people often hold onto feelings and keep them hidden for some time after bereavement.

- Third, to help the client to overcome obstacles to readjusting after a loss. This is particularly relevant to people with learning disabilities where the practical difficulties of advocating for themselves and the reality of being dependent on others can be a real block.

- Fourth, to help the client to be able to remember the deceased person at the same time as being able to live their current life without being distracted by grief.

Of course this assumes that each practitioner is going to be available to see individual clients through each goal and that having completed each one, that the work is done. In reality it is likely that we will work with people at different points in the grief process, and it is unlikely to be able to have a 'happy ending' with every psychological task being resolved, but as a framework for the management of bereavement it is helpful.

Tasks of counselling

The tasks of counselling work are helpfully outlined by Michael Jacobs (2005) and can be applied to bereavement and loss work as with other therapeutic areas. Counselling and psychotherapy sessions can help by providing a safe psychological space in which to talk about the impact of loss from this experience.

The importance of naming feelings and identifying what happens and what initiates an emotional reaction is very important in enabling people with learning disabilities to make sense of their loss. Often pictures and illustrations can inform this process if words are not the best mode of communication.

In his book *The Presenting Past* Jacobs (2005) identifies three main tasks as follows. First, to name and identify what has happened is crucial. A client may be aware of the facts of what has happened and what has changed in their immediate circumstances but can find it hard to state what the feelings are. Loss does not lend itself very easily to a vocabulary but being able to identify the feelings of being 'angry', 'sad' and 'worried' for example can connect with people in a direct cause and effect way. Jacobs states that 'Naming starts the process of owning and controlling the person's fear of what is happening to them, in their external or internal world' (Jacobs 2005, p.44).

Second, the therapeutic relationship offers clients a chance to be valued and heard as an individual who has experienced grief. Often in families someone with a learning disability can be overlooked in their own grief process, especially if other family members are grieving too. Jacobs states that a therapeutic task is to value a client's individuality and to recognize that there is a specific set of circumstances around their loss.

Third, Jacobs recognizes the value of naming feelings in sessions despite the fear that can accompany this. He points to the fact that naming feelings – saying what they are and what they relate to – can in fact reduce fear, especially when doing so does not result in their world 'collapsing'. The therapeutic task centres around working creatively with this in sessions. In terms of learning disabilities, the knowledge that life goes on, although it can be stressful, is particularly important.

Endings

The end of any therapeutic work with clients who have learning disabilities is especially important to think about. All interventions are by their nature going to be time limited and anxieties can be carried by the person doing the work about how this may affect both them and the client. There may be unconscious fears carried about abandonment and recreating loss for the client concerned. However, endings can be an opportunity for clients who have a history of abandonment or sudden endings in professional or personal relationships to experience a different ending which is planned and supported.

Sudden or unexpected endings are often a feature of people's experience. Planning endings should be part of therapeutic work and can ideally be brought into discussion from the start of any intervention. By doing this the client will know that this work will not go on forever, and planning for the ending sessions can be done so that the client can assume more control.

Many people with learning disabilities who live in supported housing have a succession of carers coming in to work with them. When staff turnover is high, such as in larger homes, this means that endings cease to have such significance as the relationships have not had the time or quality to develop enough.

The last sessions, in terms of the transferences within the therapeutic relationship, can be an opportunity for clients to have a different experience of an ending. If you are in a professional relationship with someone, the following points are important:

- If you know that you are working with someone for only a short time, let the person know this.

- If the ending is out of your control and you don't return, then phone or write to the individual and explain that you are not coming back.

- In professional endings where the work has taken place over a period of time, try to plan the ending together and recognize the work that has been achieved.

- Try not to make promises to 'keep in touch' if you cannot do this, because it may be reminiscent of parental abandonment or may create a situation where the individual feels let down.

Key points from this chapter

- Boundaries, good contracting, being explicit about confidentiality and any sharing of information has to be a part of the preparation of the therapeutic relationship.

- Endings are an important feature of the work involved as they can be a focus for the past and how things can be done differently in the therapeutic relationship.

- Some goal setting can help to focus the work that is being planned but with agreement from the client.

7

Working with Families

Introduction

When people with learning disabilities face change following bereavement, this will involve some liaising with existing or surviving family members. This may lead to the reawakening of old conflicts and repressed attitudes towards the family member with learning disabilities, and this can be hard to face especially following a new loss.

Recently the growth in systemic thinking around learning disabilities has enabled more constructive dialogues between family members and professionals which can support change. Social, religious and cultural attitudes will impact on the way that bereavement is managed for individuals and these are all important to consider when doing this work.

Within most family units there is a balance or 'homeostasis' that is maintained. When major changes occur to the structure of the family unit, the balance can be unsettled and it takes time for people to get used to the new situation. Changes such as someone moving out, someone becoming ill, or someone dying can be significant in the way that families function. Family therapy refers to these changes as being essentially structural. The boundaries that are set up to make things safe often need to be thought about again to get used to change.

Life cycle issues

Carter and McGoldrick (1985) identified that all families experience different stages in their development. These are life events and phases that are experienced by individuals within families such as birth, going to school, forming relationships, starting work, getting married, having children, retiring and eventually dying. For people with learning disabilities, some of these stages are less likely to occur for developmental or contextual reasons. In this way they can experience a loss of potential and can feel excluded from times of family ritual.

When considering the impact of bereavement and loss on people with learning disabilities, it is useful to consider how clients often have a different experience of the life cycle. Essential developmental tasks may be unavailable to people with learning disabilities such as leaving home, forming a relationship as part of an individual couple, having children and becoming grandparents. The result of this is that people with learning disabilities can experience life through other people's life stages and not their own.

In terms of bereavement there is likely to be variation in the way that families cope with grief. In his book *Family Therapy: Concepts, Process and Practice* Alan Carr (2000) outlines several points that illustrate this in families:

- There is often no intense conversation or crisis immediately after a death.

- Depression as a reaction following a bereavement is not universal.

- Not showing emotion does not necessarily mean that there will be difficulties in adjusting in the longer term.

- The quality of relationships may change within a family following bereavement. This may result in supportive relationships continuing to be supportive whereas relationships and communication which is conflictual often becomes more pronounced under the stress of bereavement.

The above points are useful to consider in terms of how families may cope following the death of a mother or father when an adult with learning disabilities is involved. Worden (2003) identifies three main factors that can influence the way that grief is managed within a family: first, he considers the function or role that the deceased person played in the family. Second, he considers the way that emotional integration of a family has been managed. Third, he says that a task must be to see 'how families facilitate or hinder emotional expression' (Worden 2003, p.152).

The dynamics that are within a family (the way that people interact with each other) can be such that shared grieving is more difficult and that individual members carry their grief in greater isolation. Rather than being 'interactional', the grief is experienced as 'individual'. It is clear that dynamics within a family are invariably set up from an early stage if there is a child with learning disabilities, as the parents and wider family unit make changes to accommodate that child's needs.

Beliefs and customs

In attempting to work effectively and understand loss and bereavement within families, it is essential to have an understanding of the context of the belief systems within each family. This will give an insight into how families approach the area of grief and loss and how that interacts with cultural attitudes to learning disabilities.

Loss felt by parents

The way that the news of having a child with any kind of disability was communicated to parents years ago reflected the social attitudes of the time. Some parents told of the experience of having a newborn baby in the 1950s and 1960s as being one that was dismissive and judgemental, where there was no support and little hope. Some parents recall being told that 'you may as well put him/her in an institution and get on with your life'.

This historical legacy has been largely forgotten about in modern times but remains part of the experience of older parents, who were given little support years ago. Parents frequently had negative experiences from medical staff. Some of the memories of treatment from years ago remains and there are still many older clients who will have stayed in institutions for a greater part of their lives.

Many parents, perhaps unintentionally, still carry the taboo of disability when they have a child with learning disabilities. Much of that may be an extension of their own fears and exposure to disabled people in their own childhood experience.

Loss of *being* parents

Many couples with learning disabilities are now able to form relationships that are loving and lasting and have the approval of others around them. This has been a shift from years ago when intimate relationships were viewed with either suspicion or extreme caution by others. The underlying belief may have been that consensual sex between people with learning disabilities was taboo or to be discouraged with regard to risk and accountability.

One parent who had an additional physical disability that prevented her from holding her baby said:

> I wanted to keep my daughter but the social workers said that I might hurt her if I dropped her so I couldn't have her with me and she went to live somewhere else. I only meet with her a couple of times each year at a children's centre. (Personal communication)

Having children in a relationship between consenting adults with learning disabilities still involves, understandably, a concern from others about the risks involved. Outcomes can be decided by parenting assessments, child development assessments, and risk procedures taking into account the wider system of support. Sexual education and the opportunity to think about what is involved are vital in such situations.

When a couple with learning disabilities have children, there is invariably a necessary focus on assessing whether or not they can look after them and a focus on risk that protects the child. Although the safety of the children involved is paramount, occasionally there can be an impact on the parents concerned. When parents who have learning disabilities have had children, they can be reluctant to seek help when needed because of a historical fear that their children will be taken into care. In such situations it can be easy for parents with learning disabilities to avoid contact with services when they actually need the support more.

Issues for older parents

It is common for people with learning disabilities who are currently between the ages of about 35 and 55 to have lived at home with their parents for many years. Having finished school, they may have moved on to a local day centre and typically to have continued attending this.

One of the positive aspects to diversifying services is that it has given people with learning disabilities more choice, and this is a good thing. For some older people, this has been a difficult transition and it has to be recognized that there can be an accompanying loss.

Day centres and social education centres are the main provider of services for skills and recreation. The positive side of these is that they can be a focus for regular social contact and, being based in the community, they are ideally placed to focus on independent living skills and accessing other resources. Many older parents have been able to maintain contact with other families that they have known for years and there is a sense of connectedness that comes from this. At a time of transition, following a family bereavement for example, the centre can be a safe place that provides a sense of continuity.

The disadvantage, however, is that people over the age of 35 may have attended centres for many years without any change. As a consequence, day centres will have been the main centre for activity and social contact, and the opportunity to have developed any social life outside of them will have been limited. Echoes of institutionalisation can appear when people have attended the same centre for 15 or more years with minimal change. Recent analysis of social policy and service planning has led to a rethink about how day care services and educational provision should be diversified to give individuals choices that best meet their needs. This has followed on from the Valuing People legislation and also consultation with advocacy groups in learning disability services. Similar movements have occurred in other countries.

Since the mid-1990s there has been a lot of change within these services due to a need for reviewing service provision. However, such services can also be hostage to budgets and changes in council delivery. For older parents when change comes, they often view this as being outside of their control, and it can happen when they themselves feel much more dependent on others. The future for their son or daughter can seem less certain and although such changes can be presented as 'opportunities', for older parents this can be confusing if there is less certainty. The future of their son or daughter can suddenly come into greater focus as well as their own future needs and this can raise existing anxieties.

In addition to this change, older parents often face decisions about their own care. Fears of the future may emerge as they witness the ageing of their son or daughter. In the context of diversifying services that are less permanent, they often worry about the potential risks that may be posed to the child who they have cared for and protected for years. The fear of handing over responsibility to care managers at the same time as recognizing their own mortality can be stressful. However, when writing about the impact of transition in later years, Jacobs (2005) comments that this 'depends on attitudes and not upon externals' indicating the reality that having a realistic yet positive and flexible approach where possible can make a difference.

Case study: Benjamin

Benjamin had lived with his father in South London for the 12 years since his mother died. Following his mum's death, Benjamin and his dad had adapted to their routine together. They did the weekly shopping, and attended the local day centre where he had kept friends for over 20 years. Benjamin had been diagnosed as being on the autistic spectrum, but he had coped well with his mum's death primarily because of the continuity that his dad had kept for him. Everything had changed, yet in his day-to-day routine very little had changed. He missed his mum but had got used to helping out and life had got back to some kind of normality reasonably soon. His receptive and spoken language was good, and he was able to maintain friendships and had a good group of friends. Some of these friends had moved in to a small supported house together and Benjamin used to go to see them every now and then at weekends.

Benjamin's dad had to carry a lot of the grief on his own but was relieved that Benjamin had coped so well. Benjamin's aunt had temporarily helped out, and it was understood that she would manage the situation if anything happened to his dad in the future.

However, when Benjamin's dad died suddenly, these plans did not work quite as well as planned. Benjamin's aunt decided that the only way to 'tidy things up' was for Benjamin to move to her family in North London, and within a couple of weeks he had moved away from his home to her house. At the same time a place became available at the house where Benjamin's friends lived but his aunt refused to think about him going there as it would unsettle him and 'he would be better off with family'.

Three months later none of his friends had had any contact with Benjamin, but he did phone to say that he had moved and he missed his friends and the social clubs he went to.

What is clear from the above case study is that on this occasion family members acted too rashly and it is unclear whose interests were being served more. Moving suddenly can be disruptive and disorientating for some people, and Benjamin's interests were not being truly considered. Friendships can be hard to maintain over even small distances if there is not regular transport, and it can be hard to start over again.

In such situations it may have been in Benjamin's best interests to have an independent advocate or to have had a stronger representation for what his wishes were, rather than it being assumed what was going to happen by his extended family.

Preparing for the future

The following factors can complicate decisions that need to be thought about.

Vulnerability factors

In assessing how to think about the future with families and clients, it may appear that there is a plan or at least some thinking about how the future will play out if a dependent person with learning disabilities has remained at home. However, this may be an assumption rather than an actual plan. It is easier to put off thinking ahead especially if there is some fear or reluctance to think about the responsibilities that may be involved for other people. Death can happen suddenly and without warning, especially in later years and sometimes even though other family members may be aware of the longer term and the potential decisions that will need to be made, it can be easier to 'put it off' rather than initiate a discussion about it.

There is also an increased risk of a surviving parent or parents becoming increasingly frail or ill and requiring care themselves. These times of transition can be emotionally and physically difficult for everyone involved.

Insufficient preparation

There can often be a denial of the future and what may be needed. It can feel easier for families to think about an indefinite time in the future rather than make plans in good time. This can also be a painful process if the family members that you assumed would be around at a time of need indicate that they don't want that responsibility.

Some families have always been determined to manage on their own maybe because of a fear of service involvement and for elderly parents this can require a rethinking around practicalities. There are also social and cultural factors or memories of how services were in the past that can make families reluctant for any external involvement.

However, there can be a strong feeling of unfinished business that can emerge as parents get older and want their responsibilities to be in order. This can often start at the age of retirement but can be triggered by illness or separation.

Managing feelings of parents

If you are a parent of a dependent adult, it can be very hard to think about the person that you care for and their own needs. There is a real concern that the way that you cared for them – your understanding of their needs and preferences – cannot continue in the way that you wished. Religious and cultural observations are essential to someone's identity and there can be a concern about whether these will continue in the way that you wished.

The whole process of anticipating the future and what will happen can be fearful as it involves letting go, and ultimately handing over responsibility to others.

These fears can be managed more easily by talking to family or friends, making contact with a voluntary organization for carers or for people with learning disabilities and voicing your fears. It is important to feel that your concerns are heard and that you are listened to. Details of services are listed at the end of this book.

Ambivalent histories

Identifying future needs for someone with learning disabilities can be fraught with complications. An individual's history may have been characterized by a time of abandonment, neglect or psychological abuse that was not identified at the time or was not recognized as being bad enough for intervention. Thoughts of the future and loss seem painful to think about. Guilt can be present from family members or an underlying feeling that love was never there in the way that it could have been. Communication in families who have had difficult pasts can make thinking about the future more difficult especially if there has been some hidden blame placed on the family member who has the disability.

Being honest about health needs

It is important to be as honest as possible about the health of a parent or carer who is likely to die within the short to medium term. This helps the individual to prepare for the fact that they may have to move and to facilitate regular visits to their ill parent or carer. Some people find hospitals to be frightening places, and care should be taken how this is done, especially if it will distress the person involved. It is probable that they will have noticed that their parent looks different, but may not have said anything for fear of making it worse. Often having someone to talk to within the immediate family can be a good way of making sense of what is happening.

Obviously it is never a good idea to pretend that everything is all right if it is clear that the parent or carer is not going to recover. If a parent, carer or loved one is very ill in a hospice, then time should be taken to explain what a hospice is and why the person is staying there. This helps the person with learning disabilities to have time to get used to the change and when the time comes to say goodbye, they should have the same opportunity as other family members to do this.

Honest discussions about health needs, both of their own health and those of people who are in the parental or caring role, are essential in helping the subsequent grief process. There may be times when people feel it is right to withhold information from people with learning disabilities but that approach really does belong to the past.

When talking to people about what is happening, it is probable that they know other people who have been in the same position as them and have faced these problems. Hospital and health care settings are much more user friendly now, and although they may not be set up to meet the needs of people with disabilities, newer hospitals can be less fearful places. The emphasis on preventative care has also increased the chance of positive outcomes.

If you are supporting someone whose parent or carer is ill and is undergoing medical treatment, the following points may help:

- Ask them what they think the situation is so that you have an awareness of their perspective on what is happening.

- Be honest but clear if this information is wrong.

- Encourage the individual to ask questions and use what they know as a basis for discussion.

Managing the effects of moving home

It is inevitable that any subsequent move that someone has to make will involve loss and sadness not only for the individual concerned but also for the wider family. However, families can be very resilient and will often have thought about how change will happen; the processes involved will have been discussed regularly with the ill or elderly parent themselves. Moving from a family home can be the end of a whole era for many people, however, and can evoke great sadness. Any change has the potential to be traumatic if managed in the wrong way. People with learning disabilities are entitled to express this sadness as much as anyone else. It is important to recognize this and not to try to make someone feel 'happy' if they are not.

It may be possible that contact is maintained with family friends and neighbours following a move. This can limit the sense that part of the past has been suddenly and irrevocably taken from the person involved. Telephone calls to and from friends and neighbours in the area can be important in the weeks after a move in keeping a link with an area if a move has been needed in the best interests of someone.

Managing when parents become ill or hospitalized

When a parent becomes suddenly ill this can be a shock both for the parent and for their son or daughter who lives with them. It can be frightening for both concerned, especially if there are no other family members around. If no preparation for respite has ever been put in place, then a whole range of assessments may be needed and it can feel very disorientating for the person involved.

The perceived difficulty with accepting change can become very difficult in these situations as support staff often become involved in day-to-day care at a point when the individual client is most resistant and experiencing a significant amount of stress that they are not able to process or manage effectively. Support staff can be the 'target' for a lot of this stress which is not easy as they are also the point of support.

Case study: Tim

Tim had attended the local day service for the past 17 years. When his Dad died 11 years ago, social services came to meet with his mum and did an assessment of both of their needs based on the current situation. Tim was 45 at the time that his dad passed away and despite having to make some changes, both he and his mum adapted well after some time into a new routine. Tim had always responded well to the way that his dad explained things to him and found certainty to be helpful to him. On a couple of occasions he had been distressed when his dad had either said one thing and done another, or when there was too much information to take in all at once.

Social services ended their direct involvement a couple of months after Tim's dad died, and for the next 20 years Tim and his mum kept themselves to themselves and appeared to be coping well. Things began to change following a chance remark made by the caretaker at the centre Tim attended, who was coming up to retirement. He had been working there for most of the time that Tim had been attending the centre and jokingly commented to him that 'You'll be retiring soon'.

Over the next couple of months Tim became fixed on this idea and decided to tell his mother that 'We are retiring, and we will be able to spend more time together.' Tim began to opt out of going to the centre on certain days of the week, and although people around him noticed that he wasn't going there so much, everyone assumed it was a phase that he was going through and that he would soon get bored at home.

Tim's mum was rather confused by the change that he had decided to make, and had begun to forget what day of the week it was now that Tim was home more. Tim had started to enjoy his semi-retirement and thought it was a 'good idea' of his to stay home and also he could 'look after' his mother. However, this became more problematic as the weeks progressed and he became more demanding of his mum, who didn't want to trouble anyone with her concerns. Tim had started to ask her why she wasn't doing the things that she used to do around the house, and began to become argumentative when they were at home.

Following one 'argument' at the weekend that he initiated with his mum, Tim lost his temper and hit his mum. When the escort noticed that his mum had a black eye she reported her concerns, leading to social services doing an emergency risk assessment.

Tim's mum was placed in emergency respite for safety and also to do further assessment on the probability of dementia. Tim continued to live at the house with a support worker coming in for 15 hours a week. He was angry that his mum had left and couldn't understand why it had happened so quickly, saying that 'she shouldn't be with those other people – she should be here with me to look after me'.

Unfortunately this type of presentation is not uncommon and reflects the complexities that clients often have with coping with change when facing loss. Any bereavement or loss can lead to a disruption to an individual's routine that can be unsettling.

It is common for families to present to services mainly at times of crisis, and this can create more problems later on. The way that change is managed can affect the longer-term outcomes. It is easy for a family system that is coping well to change, particularly when there are elderly parents, and it requires that we are all aware of vulnerability factors at such times.

Dealing with structural change

Following a death, particularly of a mother, there can often be a change in the general structure of a family and the way it is 'run'. The power in families can shift following bereavement and people with learning disabilities are often cared for by siblings, mainly sisters or female relatives.

It can be hard for everyone in this situation to get used to these changes, and to get used to being supported by someone who was a sister or brother who previously had an equal relationship with their joint parent and now has to accept their sister or brother being responsible for them. Often conversations and arrangements concerning the future are held way in advance of bereavement, but sometimes there is a lot of upheaval for everyone concerned.

There are cultural differences in the way that families approach the idea of caring for a relative with learning disabilities. Some parents expect that care will provided by a son, daughter or other relative when they are no longer alive, while it is different within other cultures.

When changes occur that affect the family structure, it is often helpful to have some systemic or family therapy sessions. Systemic psychotherapy sessions are a helpful way for people who are facing family or group change to talk about the implications of their loss. Details can be found through learning disability psychology services in your local area.

Key points from this chapter

- When working with families one has to be aware of the sensitivities to services and how when facing loss and bereavement a family may be at a vulnerable point themselves.

- It is important to be mindful of religious and cultural beliefs within families.

- Bereavement and illness within families can often precede a move and planning for an individual with learning disabilities who may be confused and distressed.

8

The Carer's Role in Bereavement

Introduction

This chapter considers the role of people identified as carers – not just immediate parents but other relatives who are carers, and people who become carers. Sometimes it can be hard to recognize when one is a carer, as many caring relationships begin in a different time and a different context.

For people with learning disabilities the 'parent' role that fitted a child may not change, but acquires a different meaning and responsibility once that person becomes an adult themselves.

It is not only parents who assume carer responsibilities. This chapter looks at the carers and the cared for in learning disabilities and how these roles can be managed when facing loss.

Knowing someone's history

Because of learning disabilities, people may not understand cognitively in the same way. Their way of processing grief can be much more complex. Often grief reactions emerge a long time afterwards and can be triggered by unrelated events tapping into someone's history which present carers may not know of.

Often, people with learning disabilities do not have the same opportunities to reflect upon their experience. Loss and change can be isolating and lonely experiences for people in these situations. It can feel tempting to say that you 'know how someone feels', but really we are never in a position to identify with anyone's experience in the same way as them. Observing how someone that you are working with or caring for is managing, being supportive and empathic are the most helpful things that we can do.

Who is a carer?

A carer can be anyone who spends time looking after someone who is too ill or disabled to care for themselves. This could be parents, siblings, children of the person being looked after or friends of the family who find themselves being drawn further into the role of looking after someone. These types of caring roles are essentially informal arrangements because they are not 'employed' through an external agency.

Sometimes people can underestimate the stress that being a carer can cause and if the individual you are caring for has behaviour that is demanding, then it can be exhausting very quickly.

Staff training needs

Offering staff training on bereavement and loss issues is an important way of informing and supporting staff who are working with vulnerable people with learning disabilities. Getting the right training and support as well as good supervision is essential when working in this area.

Carers are often the people who have to support individuals with learning disabilities who are experiencing grief and loss. Without specific training around bereavement it can be difficult to 'get it right' when helping a client that you work with around loss and grief experiences. You are, however, a witness to their distress and also to the experience that they are going through.

Supporting a client who is facing a bereavement

The following points are general guidelines that can help if you are a carer for someone facing bereavement.

Be present

The most important thing that anyone in a caring capacity can do is to be supportive and to be there for clients who are experiencing loss and bereavement. For example, if you are a support worker during a difficult loss for someone, it means paying a little bit more attention to people when they are distressed, helping out with any of the practical matters following the loss, making sure that clients have sufficient rest, and so on.

Seek out any helpful materials explaining around death and loss

Sometimes it can be helpful to involve people in creating memory resources, such as life books, photo albums, etc. (A 'life book' is a chronological account of someone's life history so far that enables people to build up a narrative of the events in their lives and the people that were/are associated with them. This may be supplemented by photographs and pictures, and is particularly helpful in reminiscence work.) However, this should be done only if the individual wants to do this and should not be imposed on them as 'a good idea'.

Avoid change if possible

At times of bereavement or major events such as changes in day care or college, it is hard to manage a lot of change at once. Communicating with the other relevant agencies involved in someone's care can help to avoid unnecessary change for someone at these times.

Support people to remember anniversaries

If someone you are caring for becomes preoccupied or distressed coming up to an anniversary, it can be helpful to involve them in an activity that will help them to remember in a positive way. This could be by visiting a favourite place or doing something that was associated with the past that they enjoyed doing. This has to be done with sensitivity though, as introducing memories without them initiating this could be unhelpful.

Encourage different social activities that the person would like

Grieving can take some time to work through but it is also important to encourage people to continue with social activities that they can join in with. It does happen following bereavement and loss that there can be a period where everything seems to change and it can be overwhelming. Joining in with social activities and groups that someone enjoys can be a welcome distraction if people wish to do so.

Be aware of your own needs

Caring for someone who is ill or someone who has been recently bereaved can be very tiring. The experience can affect our physical and psychological health and it is easy to carry unwanted stress when you are caring. If it is possible to share responsibilities then it is good to do so, and also to have the chance to talk about how you feel in a way that will not be judged. Caring for people with specific communication and behavioural needs can be particularly wearing if their behaviour is made worse by pain or other distress.

Systemic implications of a loss

Adults with learning disabilities often have different relationships with different people. Many of these relationships are formed more by chance, historical events or personal history than by choice. Although there are many adults with learning disabilities who will have lived with their family for many years, there are also a significant number (particularly older clients) who will not, and who either lived in residential services for many years or had experiences of being put into care from an early age.

The impact of experiencing loss can reach far beyond someone's immediate circle. Our own bereavements commonly are experienced within the context of immediate family who can provide a sense of connection and support to each other. In other words the family system can ideally hold and support the sense of loss felt by others. For people who have lived in residential services for many years or who have seen a succession of adult foster carers, their experience will have been different. Carers in this situation have a pivotal role in providing a sense of security to clients.

Carers are now recognized as being central to the support and care of many people with learning disabilities. The impact of this is now more recognized by government and society. This chapter considers the impact of caring for someone who has experienced a bereavement or who is going through a period of change in which they need extra emotional support.

The role of carers

The 2001 Census shows that there are about 6 million carers in UK looking after relatives, partners or friends. This is about 10 per cent of the UK population. The 2001 Census states that there are 1.9 million people who care for more than 20 hours a week although a significant amount of people will care for more than 50 hours a week; about 60 per cent of carers were women and 40 per cent were men. Carers are likely to be in the 50–59 year age range although the number of younger carers is increasing. There are greater numbers of carers in certain groups, for example the 2001 Census found that people in Bangladeshi and Pakistani communities were three times more likely to be carers.

There is evidence to suggest that there is a considerable amount of physical and psychological stress on carers especially if the caring role has been sustained for more than a year. In 2004 a study by Michael Hirst for the University of York entitled *Hearts and Minds: The Health Effects of Caring* said that the first year of caring resulted in a decline in physical health for the carer. It also drew attention to the facts that 'spouse carers' and mothers looking after a child with disabilities were most at risk of psychological distress.

National Service Framework for Mental Health and the Carers Act

In order to meet the general needs of carers, the National Service Framework for Mental Health was introduced by the UK government in 1999. As with other National Service Frameworks in the UK, this set out national standards for mental health care and the needs of carers became a part of this.

The Carers Act in 1996 highlighted the specific needs that carers can face and gave carers the right to have an assessment of their needs, whether or not a carer lives in the same property as the person that they care for. The carer's assessment covers areas such as health needs, the emotional impact of caring, asking about whether or not they are getting the right benefits, and entitlement of carers to have breaks from caring.

Caring for someone with learning disabilities

People become family carers for a variety of reasons. Sometimes it can be from a sense of loyalty and duty; it can also be because no one else feels able to take on the responsibility. Often the interaction between the carer and the person cared for can be affected when the status of the relationship changes. The following questions can be pertinent at these times:

- What is or was the carer's existing relationship with the client like?
- What were the circumstances of the client having a carer?

- At what stage in the life cycle did the client experience the loss?
- At what stage is the carer in the life cycle?

Carers who look after people with learning disabilities often face these issues when managing change and helping clients to get used to an altered situation when mourning someone that they have known or loved. As carers supporting clients in loss and bereavement, it is common for a client's grief to stay with us. It is important at such times to separate out what are our own feelings and grief and what are theirs. Sometimes there is a concern that we may be unconsciously communicating some feelings about not wanting to 'go there' as it can trigger emotions in the relationship.

Long-term foster placements

Some people with learning disabilities have long-term adult fostering placements where they have lived for many years and appear to be happy. Such placements can over time create a sense of family that is nurturing and meets the needs of the individuals involved. Living in such a placement can be an ideal way of giving a sense of home, although it can also be difficult to manage if a placement comes to an end, especially if there has not been much long term planning.

Other people in the foster placement may have been placed there with little consultation, but the situation had seemed to work well for many years. Sometimes an elderly carer suddenly becomes unwell and requires hospitalization. Strong bonds, similar to that of living with an elderly parent, can be established. It can be assumed that the person actually being called 'mum' is a blood relative. However, following a death of a foster carer in an adult placement the placement has to be changed.

The person with learning disabilities then becomes confused and is taken back to earlier memories of being displaced or being moved suddenly. This can reawaken fears of abandonment if managed in the wrong way.

Case study: Nathan and Daniel

Nathan and Daniel were aged 43 and 40 and were long-term friends. They lived with an adult carer, Josie, in the north of England and had been with her for the past 18 years following the closure of a local residential home in the city. Initially Nathan and Daniel had both had a history of 'challenging behaviour'. The carer thought that having both Nathan and Daniel would be easier in some ways as they 'got on well and seemed to be friends'.

Services were keen to place them both at the same time; they were placed together and attended the day centre together for five days a week.

When Josie became ill, both Nathan and Daniel went into temporary respite care. This lasted for two months prior to Josie dying. Following the funeral, the subject of Nathan and Daniel's longer-term placement became a central concern and it was assumed that they would find another foster placement together. At this point, however, the social worker who was working with Daniel pointed out that it should not be assumed that they wanted to be together and suggested getting an advocate involved who would be external to all other decision making.

Over the next two months what transpired was that Nathan and Daniel respected each other but wanted to live away from each other for a while. It had been assumed that they would want to be together but it was only with the intervention of the advocate that these assumptions were challenged.

Supporting people in residential care facing loss and bereavement

There are two aspects to consider when supporting people who are experiencing bereavement in residential care: how to manage ongoing contact with the family when someone has died, and how to consider and manage attitudes to bereavement within teams where there can be different attitudes and beliefs around death and bereavement.

Relationships with family

The relationships that staff teams have with families or the next of kin of people who live in residential care can be difficult. Clients who live in supported housing have all sorts of reasons why they are being cared for. Staff teams can find it hard to maintain transparent working relationships with wider family member due to the complexities of family dynamics. The result of this can be that distrust is set up, especially when there are systemic changes within the family, and it can be hard to adjust the relationship with staff.

It can seem that at these times it is hard for staff teams supporting someone who has family nearby to get it right. Some families become over-involved and can accentuate existing disagreement with staff teams from a need to assuage their guilt or other feelings towards the side of the family that the individual is part of.

Staff teams also have to work within the guidelines set out by the organization they are employed by. Policies are there to give consistency but can appear to be rigid to wider family who may not have had daily contact with the individual concerned for some time. At times of grieving, conflicts like this can become magnified and if managed wrongly can lead to further disagreement and resentments. The boundaries that have to be in place through a duty of care to clients may protect clients but can feel like a further source of conflict to some grieving relatives who may not understand the need for such policies.

Working in a team with different attitudes to loss and bereavement

It is common for staff teams to reflect different work and life experiences as well as diverse cultures and beliefs around life and death. Conflicting attitudes may be voiced following the death of a client. The following are a few guidelines to bear in mind when approaching staff discussions:

- Recognize that we all have different attitudes to loss and bereavement. Try not to impose your values on others as they may wish to emulate your example without thinking through what they believe themselves. Recognize that clients have different needs and may have different beliefs.

- Remember that it is always good to review existing guidelines. Recognize that they are there for consistency and to avoid conflict and competition but can be a shared statement of policy.

- Respect the beliefs of clients and families we care for. Remember that it is also important to include the right to have no specific beliefs.

- Remember that staff training is important to support the team at times of loss and to engender some empathy from others around you. Recognize that the impact on staff can be significant if they have to support people around bereavement indefinitely and can lead to 'compassion fatigue'.

- Respect the fact that everyone has their own relationship with the deceased person.

End of an adult fostering relationship

Adult fostering is common in being a viable option for looking after people with learning disabilities. Adult fostering arrangements can continue for a number of years and can afford a feeling of family life on a semi-permanent basis that may not be available in other ways. It can feel as if such arrangements could go on for ever but eventually carers become older and people have to move on.

When fostering ends it can bring up a lot of rejection and grief from those who are being cared for.

Key points from this chapter

- We all bring different fears and issues when caring for someone with learning disabilities. In teams it is important to communicate a consistent message to clients and their families.

- It is important to consider the role of carers in terms of their age and their life experience.

- Self care is always important for carers of people living with learning disabilities.

- In the UK every new carer is entitled to a carer's assessment of need.

9

Working with Clients who have Additional Communication Needs

Language and meaning

> Communication difficulties that erect a social barrier add considerable complexity to the process of achieving a consolidated identity. (Wilson 2003, p.115)

One of the most important aspects of any bereavement is the ability to be able to convey the information in a clear and sensitive way. It requires that whoever is communicating news does so in a way that is understood and with sensitivity to the person concerned. Thinking back on our personal experiences of hearing sad news following our own bereavements, it is common to remember where we were, who gave us the news, whether it was face to face, over the phone, by email or letter.

In learning disabilities it has been found that more than 50 per cent of people have some form of communication difficulty (Kerr *et al.* 1996). This presents a major problem regarding how grief is talked about and understood and it highlights the need for communication around this sensitive area to be clear and unambiguous. Having additional communication difficulties can add to the experience of isolation that is felt by many people with learning disabilities.

The way that we receive news of loss and the manner in which it is explained can be an indicator of how we will respond in the following days and weeks. This inevitably involves using language that is understood. Talking through the experience and making sense of what happens with another person is therapeutic and if there are misunderstandings we rely on being able to communicate these to others. Our ability to reflect and find meaning over following months whether by talking it through with family and friends, writing, listening to religious or spiritual messages and teachings or having some therapy sessions enables us to find insight into what has happened.

People with a learning disability often have problems with receptive and spoken language. Finding the words to say how we feel following grief can be hard enough when we have a breadth of vocabulary and can find comfort in the subtleties of words that ease our sadness. The accompanying loss of language that people with learning disabilities face can lead to an experience of 'disempowered grief' where it is harder to express how one feels. When this happens, other tools can help clients in the mourning process.

Clients who have little or no language will experience intense feelings of loss. The lack of spoken communication can be extremely stressful. Finding ways around this when facing loss is vital to clients who may internalize emotional pain. It can also affect the work that is done in any therapeutic relationship. To quote Shula Wilson again:

> When a client's communication is impaired the therapist's anxiety is heightened: it leaves the therapeutic dyad exposed, bereft of the protective cover of language which, as well as being a means of exchange and interaction, also offers defensive options. (Wilson 2003)

Identifying non-verbal change

Reactions to bereavement can present in behavioural terms for some clients who do not have alternative ways to express their grief. They can also be expressed through body language, facial expression, levels of attentiveness or increased arousal. When there is change in the person's situation this can often lead to being more irritable and anxious, with an increase in behaviours that may have previously been managed much better. It sometimes appears that there is a regression in response to change.

Signs of distress may include:

- isolating self more than usual
- self-harm not previously seen
- changes in mood and behaviour
- sleeping problems.

This chapter outlines some of the difficulties that clients with reduced language skills may experience following bereavement and loss. It suggests other tools that can be helpful in such circumstances.

Behavioural changes

Changes in behaviour following bereavement and loss are common and are mainly as a result of the reaction to the change itself. Changes in routine, environment and the absence of familiar people can be deeply distressing. Behavioural change can result from not having the vocabulary to express feelings or not having the time to process complicated information and alterations to routine etc.

It is necessary when people are facing loss and change to consider what the 'difficult' or different behaviour is communicating about that individual's distress. Changes in behaviour that follow bereavement can be challenging for professionals who know the client(s) concerned as it can indicate the level of stress and distress from the client. People with autism, for example, may find the stress of loss to be particularly hard.

Echolalia

'Echolalia' is the repeating or echoing of what is said by another person. It is common in many people who have autism and is characterized by a lack of spontaneity in language. During bereavement echolalia may become more noticeable as someone is working to accept the facts of what has happened and feels the need to rehearse what has been explained to them, sometimes a long time after they originally heard it.

Finding a way to communicate what happened but being unable to move away from certain key repetitive phrases can become a fixed permanent feature of how one communicates. Not having the cognitive ability to move away from the focus of emotional distress can be limiting and can reinforce an intensity of emotional pain on a daily basis, and people may appear to get stuck in a perpetual cycle of grief.

Involving speech and language therapy

Speech and language therapists have a very important role to play in facilitating loss and bereavement and can work closely with behavioural practitioners, psychologists and other members of multidisciplinary teams. Speech and language therapists are in an ideal position to advise on a person's level of comprehension. They can assess the best way that an individual can express themselves as well as give advice about how to facilitate this. This differs for each individual client and is dependent not only on physical factors but also on emotional ones following bereavement.

The importance of existing relationships is another factor here. It could be that an individual is currently known to a speech and language therapist. However, speech and language therapists are unlikely to become newly involved in the period after bereavement as a person experiencing loss may not be in the right psychological place to have a new professional working with them.

Instead they are more likely to give advice to family or staff teams on how to present information to the individual(s) concerned in a way that is easier to understand. This may also provide advice on the best way to express their feelings. The emphasis is not on acquiring new skills but on ways that can facilitate expressions of feelings that are accessible.

Speech and language therapists may help the family and carers by gathering information about the way that an individual communicates. This can be helpful in thinking about strategies that can help the individual concerned. This in turn can reduce the anxiety felt by the family and carers about whether or not they are helping in the best way they can.

Joint work between speech and language therapists, psychologists, nursing, counselling, psychotherapy and behavioural support practitioners can be the most effective way of supporting clients. This can be for an extended period although any involvement is often dependent on resources and need.

Makaton®

Makaton is a system involving signs and speech in daily living and communication with some people who have learning disabilities. It involves gesture, speech and hand signs. It was devised by speech and language therapists in Derbyshire and encourages communication around everyday items and feelings. It is based on signs from British Sign Language and its main aim is to encourage the link between sign and speech in an interactional way. Makaton involves the use of pictorial symbols that can support communication in a number of settings to encourage the development of communication. From its beginnings it was used widely as being an easily understandable and usable communication system and was integrated into everyday activities for many people who attended day services and in some residential settings.

Makaton is now widely used in community settings and has enabled many people to develop better communication skills. As a language and communication tool it is invaluable. For many people with learning disabilities in particular it can be frustrating trying to communicate emotions, actions and wishes to others especially if this is in a stressful or rushed environment. Makaton is also used as a communication device for people with learning disabilities who are deaf.

Using Makaton to communicate emotions around loss and bereavement

Makaton can be used effectively to express emotions. It has also been integrated into expression through dance and movement.

There are specific signs for emotions such as 'happy', 'sad', 'angry', 'frightened' and so on which can be effectively used to communicate events related to death, change and loss. The following case study illustrates this.

Case study: Errol

Errol used Makaton as his main support for communication. He had a degree of hearing loss and some behavioural problems. He found that Makaton helped him to communicate to others how he was feeling and, especially when he was experiencing stress, he used signs to tell people what was happening in his life and how he felt about it.

Following a period of illness, his main carer (his sister) had decided that she needed to have some support and was arranging for him to have one night a week at a local respite care unit, Willow House. She has explained this to him and identified some key signs that he would find helpful to use (sister – house – 'W house' – eat – tea – sleep – bed – happy – sad – angry).

Through having a vocabulary to explain what was happening, Errol was able to communicate and elicit some support around his feelings, building up a narrative about what was going to happen therefore giving a greater sense of being involved and saying what he felt. This was backed up by a picture chart that showed the related symbols to the signs.

The use of signs to support Errol meant that he had a greater sense of being part of the change rather than it happening to him passively. Through Makaton he could communicate more, therefore lessening the threat that change posed and the associated loss that this can bring.

Implications of using Makaton

The following points should be borne in mind:

- Makaton is an effective aid to understanding, although it has to be used sensitively when communicating news of death and loss.

- When communicating sad news, it is important to do so in a way that is clear and where there can be no ambiguity about the meaning of what is being said. Eye contact is important and being able to assess whether or not what was said has been understood.

- It is also important to be supportive and aware of the impact of this on the person who is signing.

- Makaton signing is an addition to spoken language rather than a substitution.

Talking Mats®

Talking Mats is a useful tool and communication aid that helps people who have difficulties in building up a narrative or story of what has happened. It also provides a structured framework within which to talk about a subject. It is primarily a visual aid and has been effectively used with clients who have learning disabilities, dementia and aphasia.

Symbols are created using a range of communication symbols produced by the BoardMaker software program. The mat is a darker background onto which the symbols can be placed. Symbols are organized into three main sections from left to right and each symbol is selected by the client themselves. One section (on the left of the board) is for the topic of discussion, the middle section is for emotions that relate to the situation, and the right-hand side of the board had influences on the issue, both positive and negative. Through discussion or 'interview' with a facilitator, the individual concerned is able to show emotions relating to an event (in this case illness or change caused by loss and bereavement) and its wider positive and negative impact on them as individuals.

Further infomation about Talking Mats products can be found on the internet at www.talkingmats.com. It seemed to me (having used Talking Mats with a client who was experiencing a lot of change at one point in his life) that it is a creative way to build on existing resources and has greater relational value than individual picture cards that may have previously been used instead.

Hearing loss

Losing one's hearing can complicate the process of loss and grieving as it is a loss in itself. Hearing loss is usually associated with increasing age, but there is a higher incidence of hearing difficulties in adults with learning disabilities. Added to a greater incidence of behavioural problems, experiencing hearing loss can complicate the experience of grieving when facing bereavement.

Hearing loss can affect speech and the way that people with learning disabilities interact in social situations. Specialist hearing therapists and audiologists are rare in learning disabilities and so the wait for treatment and assessment in the UK is long.

In experiencing loss, having a hearing loss can be an additional barrier to working through grief. It is also misunderstood in terms of how best to communicate with someone. Referral to an audiology department and further work with either an audiologist or hearing therapist can help to identify any hearing loss or other complications such as tinnitus ('ringing in the ears').

Sight loss

For people with learning disabilities who are losing their sight, there is an extra degree of adapting involved to maintain independence and to ensure continuity. The majority of adults with learning disabilities do not have regular sight tests and this, as with anyone, can lead to greater risks of reduced vision and sight problems in the future. For people with more severe learning disabilities, it may be less obvious that sight loss is happening over time. As people with learning disabilities are living longer, the need for age-related eye testing is just as necessary. It is easy for confusion or apparent lack of concentration of previously enjoyable hobbies to be mistaken when it is actually sight change that is the cause.

Sight loss and hearing loss can be monitored and checked at regular intervals to prevent further unnecessary decline. When facing more advanced sight loss, if someone is registered as being blind, this can be associated with depression just as other losses and it can lead to loss of function and independence. Finding an optician who can meet the needs of someone with learning disabilities is also a priority when helping people.

Creative therapies

The creative therapies hold a very important role in the therapeutic lives of people with learning disabilities. Music, dance, drama and art are all effective at helping people to communicate and can provide a vehicle for self-expression that is not always available through words. Just as in other talking therapy relationships, the music, dance, drama or art therapy relationships are very significant and transferences can emerge through the expressed content of the work.

In managing loss and grief, music is often said to be a part of our everyday experience of reminiscence. Particular songs or pieces of music can evoke strong memories. Music can also transcend 'language', communicating feeling without words. Improvisation can help to access the unconscious at work; if this is focused around a sad or mournful piece of music that someone is actively taking part in this can be cathartic.

Similarly the representations of colour and form often reveal how someone is coping and managing their grief and loss. For any creative arts therapist, supervision to manage the process of the work and one's own feelings is essential. In dance therapy, there is an understanding that the body and mind are inseparable and interact with each other in unity to express emotions.

Feedback to staff and family members who are directly caring for someone in the hours and days after a session is also important in being mindful of the impact of this work on mood and behaviour. People with learning disabilities have found a huge area of expression in the arts, establishing theatre, dance and music groups and showing at some exhibitions.

Therapeutic relationships formed through creative therapies are an important way of facilitating feeling for people who may not be able to communicate otherwise. Contacts for further resources on creative arts interventions and their role in helping loss, bereavement and expression especially for non-verbal clients are listed at the end of this book.

Dementia and learning disabilities

Dementia is a condition that affects and interferes with communication. The effect on communication will depend on the type and stage of dementia. Dementia can have a major impact on how people process their knowledge of bereavement and change. Dementia can be seen as a loss in itself, characterized by loss of memory and function. It is also a condition that will lead to death in the long term, although the rate at which this happens will depend on a number of factors. It can have a major impact on family, friends and staff of those involved.

As health care has improved since the 1950s, and become more accessible, people with learning disabilities can expect to live much longer than a generation ago. This brings with it an increased likelihood of experiencing long-term degenerative conditions such as dementia. There are different forms of dementia, but Alzheimer's disease is the most common one associated with older age, and results in progressive loss of brain tissue.

The Alzheimer's Society outlines symptoms of dementia as including:

- increasing difficulty in completing everyday tasks
- loss of memory and concentration
- deterioration in speech and having difficulty in finding the right words
- behavioural and mood changes
- confusion and disorientation about times; places and changes
- difficulty in sorting out everyday problems.

Quite often in learning disabilities, the early signs of dementia can be overlooked. Loss of memory in the early stages can be attributed to stress or people 'not quite being themselves'. Maybe someone who has been in a service for years may have had a quirky way of communicating that was taken for granted, or there may be a number of new staff who may not be able to assess change over such a long period of time.

As professionals working with people with learning disabilities, one of the fundamental areas of care that we need to know is how someone communicates best. Based on our knowledge of the individual, we are in a better situation to be able to assess any changes that we observe and can highlight any changes that we have noticed in terms of behaviour or communication.

The risk of Alzheimer's disease occurring in people with Down syndrome notably increases past the age of 50. This has been attributed to chromosomal and genetic factors that are more pronounced in this group. Knowing that there is an increased risk of memory and communication being affected in older age in this group means that we can be more aware of it and the potential loss involved. However, developing dementia in later years is not inevitable in people with Down syndrome.

The following signs can indicate that dementia may be in its early stages:

- A loss or change in short-term memory and not being able to remember names or familiar routines.
- Changes in communication, such as loss of engagement, and a general reduction of skills, such as not joining in with activities as much as before.
- Difficulty in concentrating and an increased risk of becoming lost and disorientated.
- A general decline in being able to orientate, resulting in getting lost more easily.
- An increased need for prompting around memory and general functions or routines.
- Becoming easily distressed very quickly with behavioural change and crying.

As dementia progresses, it is common for people to grieve for relatives who have died many years ago when they had seemingly got over the loss. It can be confusing to know how to respond, especially if this loss predated the client's history or notes on file.

How this becomes more of a loss for clients

Staff and family will have to live with witnessing the person's loss of function and it can be distressing to see how the individual changes over time. However, a more active engagement process with maintaining skills and function can help. Observing this and any changes can help.

Although strategies can be in place to help people we care for, it may take time for these to work. In the meantime we can be left holding a responsibility for their well-being. Good supervision and staff support within teams is key to this.

Key points from this chapter

- Talking about our experiences can help when managing bereavement and loss. As many people with learning disabilities do not have the opportunity to do this in the same way, it is important to think about the best way for them to communicate their loss.

- Creative therapies such as dance, drama, music and art can all be helpful in expressing grief following bereavement and it is important to be mindful of what is being expressed in this work even if it is several years following a loss.

- Being aware of an individual's communication needs and what already helps them when communicating is the key to facilitating their grief.

10

Role of Supervision

Introduction

In all therapeutic work, supervision is an integral part of the work in providing a space to reflect on the relationship established between the practitioner and client. Supervision is provided for counselling, nursing, psychology, occupational therapy, speech and language therapy, residential and day care work among others. This chapter outlines the main areas that can present during supervision and how it can be a focus for practitioner support, trainee development and wider thinking. It also discusses why supervision can be a difficult process for anyone involved in supporting people with learning disabilities around loss.

Why supervision work in learning disabilities is essential

Working in areas of disability can be potentially filled with anxieties for clinicians, especially those who have not experienced much bereavement and loss work. It can be distressing to witness someone else's distress. If clinicians are relatively new to the area of learning disabilities, they may be worried about not being understood or making things worse by misunderstanding what the situation is or becoming caught up in some staff or family dynamics that are around the client.

Supervision can help the practitioner or trainee understand themselves and the clients they are working with better. Bereavement and loss can be areas that some practitioners have less experience in, for example, if they previously worked with other client groups. Having a supportive professional relationship with a supervisor who is experienced in aspects of disability and mental health is essential to the work in hand and to the practitioner doing the work.

Good supervision can facilitate clear thinking around the dynamics of the work and its practicalities as well as how the work can link in with other professionals' involvement. As learning disabilities work often involves both a systemic and a multidisciplinary focus this can be essential.

Without good supervision both the practitioner and client can be exposed: the practitioner can be left with feelings of uncertainty and doubting professional self-worth as well as transferential and countertransference anxieties. The client can potentially be left exposed too if their practitioner does not have the confidence to see the work through or is unsupported, carrying too much of the client's distress.

Establishing the contract

Depending on the professional context in which someone is working there will be difference in establishing a contract for supervision around case work involving learning disabilities. Hawkins and Shohet (2007) identify different types of supervision as follows:

- *Tutorial supervision*, where the educative function of the work is highlighted and usually linked in to the development and goals from a course.

- *Training supervision*, where there is a skills learning role inherent in the relationship.

- *Managerial supervision*, where the line management and clinical supervision components are held within the same professional relationship.

- *Consultancy supervision*, where the supervisor has no direct day-to-day responsibility for the work of the supervisee but who becomes someone with whom they can discuss issues relating to the work. This often becomes focused on wider concerns relating to the work and the context which it takes place in.

Establishing a supervision contract is likely to be negotiated between the two people involved in the supervision and should be drawn up following discussion and reflection from both parties.

Things to think about in contracts involving learning disabilities work would include the following:

- The frequency of meetings and whether more regular supervision would reflect the potential depth and needs of the counsellor or practitioner and client.

- The boundaries around confidentiality and when it may be necessary for a supervisor to seek extra advice if necessary from someone in the organization that the work relates to.

- Whether supervision is one to one or in a small group setting.

- Lines of accountability and the role of the supervisor in maintaining this particularly with regard to risk.

- The model of work that is being used and how this may impact on the client.

- Which particular code of practice is being used by the practitioner and how this can affect the work in terms of appreciation and observance of ethical codes and practice guidelines.

Functions of supervision

Kadushin and Harkness (2002) identify three main functions of supervision and the supervisory relationship: the *educative* or formative, *supportive* or restorative and the *managerial* or normative. These are outlined below with reference to the work that supervisees may face as part of the work:

Educative or formative

> I thought that I knew how to approach this work and expected it to be quite pedestrian but the learning came from the interaction with the clients themselves. (Trainee counsellor)

Working in learning disabilities is likely to be a new area for many people new to therapeutic work, although many supervisees will have had some previous experience if in a caring role. Some contextual knowledge around learning disabilities is helpful at this point and how the interventions made can have a direct impact on clients either by the words used, the actions that can precede a referral to the work or the consequences of the therapy. There is also an opportunity to reflect on responses and reactions to the client and what they bring. It is important in supervision to hear this and to not jump to any conclusions.

Supervision is a useful forum within which to explore the way that interpretations can be framed. As people with learning disabilities may have some difficulty in understanding and making use of certain interpretations, it can be helpful to suggest ways around linking events with people who the client has in their immediate life or making links between them. The key learning point for supervisees in this way is around communication, that is the wording used and the non-verbal communication that can be present in the session. It can also be helpful to consider what was said in the session with the client and how this connects to emotions that someone experiences.

It is equally important to begin thinking with supervisees about what they were feeling when they were with clients during loss. Many supervisees may defend their own feelings in supervision, maybe fearing that showing their own vulnerabilities would be a cause for concern. Communicating that it is necessary to have the ability to be self-reflective as a tool in the work can help supervisees to effect deeper interactive work that goes beyond outcome measures.

Finally, the educative function can be seen in an exploration of the dynamics of the relationship as reported by the supervisee following the session with the client. Being aware of these dynamics revealed in the transference can be especially significant to the work.

Supportive or restorative

> Before I did my counselling training I was a support worker and felt a bit helpless when I was on shift with clients that were upset. I didn't have time to talk to them for long enough. (Trainee psychologist)

The supportive function of supervision takes account of the impact of the work which can be challenging. It is hard to foster and maintain a therapeutic relationship where you are having to hold and witness the distress of grief and the awareness of a history of compound losses.

Managerial or normative

> The case that I took on in my learning disabilities nursing placement had made me feel nervous in case I did the wrong thing. My client was very anxious and depressed and I was relieved to be able to discuss it in supervision and know that the policies were there to protect both me and the patient I was working with. (Trainee psychologist)

The managerial component of supervision includes the aspect of professional development. There is likely to be a component of continuing professional development in evaluating aspects of work and assessment of progress. In terms of supervising bereavement and loss work in any capacity, there is an often unstated expectation of ensuring the safety of clients and staff working with them. There is likely to be an expectation of working in an ethical way in line with organizational policies as well as maintaining standards of work.

Issues that often present in learning disabilities supervision

There are certain common themes and concerns that present more frequently in supervision from trainees that may be unfamiliar with the client group. Working therapeutically with adults who have learning disabilities can highlight challenges for practitioners that can be usefully explored in supervision. The following areas are examples of this.

Power
Sometimes the impact of the imbalance of power in the life of someone with learning disabilities can feel overwhelming, especially to practitioners relatively unfamiliar with the context of learning disabilities work. This can be social, cultural and institutional and can involve adapting a theoretical model of loss to take into consideration wider systemic and analytic concepts. It can also affect trainees and practitioners when thinking around the wider implications of our own lives. The question of 'what if' is never far from the surface in this area of work.

Practitioners are sometimes motivated to work in learning disabilities because of a family experience or through holding a particular faith or belief. Thinking of the dynamics of power can bring questions around our own role and how we play it out. These dynamics in turn can present in the transferences or representations in the relationships we have with clients and others around them.

Overprotective or defensive with client material
Sometimes because a client's material or presentation affects us personally and, perhaps, more than we expected, there can be a sense of wanting to protect clients' material by minimizing its impact.

Alternatively there can be a wish to avoid certain details out of a desire to protect the client or out of guilt about talking about their personal information. Also there can be times when it is hard to identify what the real issues are because our own identification with the client can be strong.

It can take time to work through these issues but it is important to do so in order for clarity to emerge around the work and for the interpersonal nature of what can happen to be explored.

Holding difficult and sensitive material

The following are examples of where there can be an extra pressure around holding difficult material.

- Uncovering systematic and institutional abuse: sometimes as work progresses, it becomes clear that abuse may be taking place. Obviously the necessary steps have to be put into place to ensure that a situation involving a client or clients is made safe and the necessary authorities are alerted. It is important to make such cases examples where there are exceptions to confidentiality and this extends to supervision where there is a risk involved.

- Tasks of bereavement being more complex: inevitably there are going to be times when a bereavement case which leads to change for a client's life will be more complex where there are mental health and/or learning disabilities involved. Supervision is a good space to be able to work through these complexities.

- Holding the 'not knowing': sometimes in supervising learning disabilities cases there is an element of 'not knowing' either the circumstances of someone's current situation or more often not knowing individuals' pasts for example if records were not kept in the past. The 'not knowing' can be a frustrating dynamic in the work but it is often present when working with new or previously not known clients.

- Holding responsibility: supervision requires that the supervisor holds a degree of responsibility for the clinical work and this can be difficult, especially if there is not a clear further line of accountability. Having a clear system in place cuts down that risk.

- Politics of organizations can impact on work and funding: supervision is also difficult if there are politics or changes in funding that can affect the supervision work. At an organizational level, when there is change, this can affect the consistency of supervision and can result in a change in supervisors which is difficult for practitioners to manage, creating a disruption that may be a parallel process to that of the practitioner and the client.

• Burnout and stress can be carried by the worker: on occasions the context in which the client is living and the practitioner is working can be a distraction which presents in supervision.

Difficulties in obtaining appropriate supervision around bereavement and loss

Part of working with adults with learning disabilities if you are in a profession where you encounter people's experience of loss but are not directly talking about it or managing it is how to access it outside of the tasks required of the role. Some staff are left feeling helpless that although they are doing the job that they are doing that they do not have the skills or support necessary for managing loss. Staff can often be told that helping with bereavement and loss issues is not within their remit but this does not stop it becoming a part of the work and, in turn, it becomes a central issue for the staff concerned.

Diverting material away from loss

It is easy and, perhaps, understandable to divert any type of supervision away from the concept of loss. Perhaps this is because the focus of your work is different from this or it may be because the loss expressed is too difficult to think about if your task is different. Many jobs in learning disabilities can focus on the task in hand at the expense of recognizing the wider needs or distress around loss that is being communicated. Staff may also be uncomfortable that when they are with clients they are feeling as if they are de facto therapists and feel unprepared for this.

An important part of good supervision is to be able to help the person you are supervising to identify where the blocks are in the work that they are doing with the individual client concerned. These blocks can include the following:

• Finding it hard to separate out the task from what the client wants to talk about.

- Finding it hard to 'hold' the loss that clients leave us with. Sitting with loss can be very hard especially if it cannot be easily expressed in language.

- Not wanting to acknowledge emotionally difficult feelings within yourself.

- Feeling bad about getting irritated with the client when not in the right frame of mind, and finding it hard to work with clients.

- Acknowledging transference, such as who you may represent to the client.

- Finding it hard to motivate a client who has had a recent bereavement.

- Feeling unsupported.

- Feeling that the client is not being supported enough by the organization.

Encouraging self-reflection

Part of the supervision process especially for trainees, but applicable to everyone working in this area, is the importance of self-reflection: how the work can impact on us as individuals both personally and professionally.

Being honest about the blocks that we carry in relation to the therapeutic work and the clients themselves can be a deepening part of the process that can be explored in supervision. This can sometimes be seen as threatening as it can encourage us to think about aspects of the work or aspects of ourselves that may have been 'split off' or intolerable to think about, but this is part of the supervision process that has to be encouraged for good self-reflective working.

Working with trainees

It is necessary for trainee clinical psychologists to do a placement with adults with learning disabilities as part of their training as well as placements in older adults, child and adult services. This is linked into the practice teaching at the training university, typically a series of lectures on theory and practice. However, the actual practice with clients as part of a learning disabilities team can be different from what people expected. Comments such as 'I expected to be bored or depressed', 'Initially I thought it was something I would have to just get through', 'I didn't expect it would take so long to set things up' and 'I felt isolated' are typical of the anticipation and fears that trainees can face.

It is important in learning disabilities work, particularly around bereavement, loss and change, to recognize that there are limits to how much can be achieved. Supervisees can often expect to achieve more than is possible especially at the start of an intervention. Planning and realistic expectations of outcomes and process are important parts of the work so that the referred client has a good outcome and the trainee can feel as if the work they did made a difference.

Supervision is likely to focus around both behavioural work and/ or talking therapy cases that focus more on individual loss but often involve some systemic thinking. This may involve a greater degree of liaison with other staff and carers involved in someone's care.

Common challenges for trainees
The following problems are often found while doing a learning disabilities placement:

- Working within a shortened time frame which can limit the depth of the work and the necessary time to do induction and the subsequent setting up of the work can be frustrating.

- In practical terms it can be difficult to contact the people involved with a client who has been referred. Many trainees are at placement for only a couple of days a week. With many staff being in residential or other services, it can often take several weeks to contact the necessary people.

- Bereavement and loss may be new areas for trainees and this can hold a lot of fears.

- It is common to feel overwhelmed by the material, especially if there is an over-identification with the clients and/or the material.

- Working with clients who have limited language can be hard and can feel as if it slows the work down, consequently leaving trainees feeling deskilled, especially if this means rethinking how to do the work.

- Systemic aspects may be new for them and there may be added difficulty if loss, bereavement or transition come on top. Working within a wider system can be a new experience for trainees in practice and it can take time to consider all the parties involved.

- When a staff member leaves, it can be a time for reflective thinking, for preparing for endings and anticipating that there may be unresolved issues in relation to clients who have a special bond with them. These endings should be prepared for as far as possible.

- Power issues may be of concern and can leave trainees feeling unsure or uncomfortable, especially if working with clients who are of the same age as them. This can accentuate the difference between what has been taught and what actually can happen in the therapeutic setting. It is important to explore this in supervision.

Despite these potential difficulties, working with people with learning disabilities can challenge trainees or other people new to the area to work in a more creative way and to think about the therapeutic relationship differently to maximize the use to the clients and also to promote the skills and ideas of the trainee.

Supervising trainee counsellors

Whereas learning disabilities is a required placement in psychology training, it is comparatively rare to do a learning disabilities placement when training to be a counsellor. The British Association for Counselling and Psychotherapy (BACP) does not currently have a specialist interest group for learning disabilities. Typically a trainee counsellor working in a learning disabilities setting would have some prior knowledge of learning disabilities work and may have worked in a day care, residential setting or a support worker role.

Supervising residential staff

Although the majority of supervision for residential staff will be about practice-based issues and will be goal orientated linked in to appraisal outcomes, bereavement is an area which may not be covered as much as other areas. It is important to recognize the effect that bereavement and working with vulnerable clients can have on staff. Night staff are particularly at risk of encountering emergency situations that can lead to hospital admissions and being on their own to manage it, despite arrangements being made for on-call or sleep-in staff.

Adequate supervision not only involves practical and organizational aspects but also should incorporate emotional support while there are vulnerable clients to look after.

Different organizations have different policies and it is always advisable to keep these up to date to fit the needs of clients and the staff teams that work for them to ensure that bereavement issues are talked about when needed.

Supervising day care staff

One of the things that I think about since I've moved on from working there was how much change those clients have had. I don't know how I would manage it now... I suppose we got used to it when I was there but I see now what effect it had on some of them. (Retired day centre worker)

Day care can be a focus for a lot of loss and bereavement. Day services have changed now in many areas of the UK and taken on a more community resource feel linking with local services and colleges. However, day services still remain a key part of provision and form a central part of care for people on an ongoing basis.

Staff who work in day services come into contact with many service users who are facing change and loss, yet supervision is often focused around policy and procedures. The work can be very energetic and forward looking, yet there are areas that are not often discussed, such as the dynamics of dependency that can emerge in a teaching, training or key worker relationship. Many staff and clients in this area of provision have been part of services for years and have strong working relationships with each other. Change can be difficult to manage, especially if some of the more permanent staff move on.

Aspects of the above points can be usefully explored in supervision and there should be a place to explore the presenting losses that many clients experience.

'Death and loss' for trainees

The catalogue of losses that many people with learning disabilities experience can be a real shock for trainees of all disciplines coming into this area of work. Although there are comprehensive training modules on courses prior to doing direct clinical work, actually meeting clients who have had a history of significant loss can be hard and can require some reflective thinking about what impact this has on them as individuals and the services that manage them.

Communication is another area that can prove to be problematic, especially in relation to attachment, and it can be hard to form therapeutic relationships for anything more than a few months before trainees leave to go on another placement. However, it is possible to do some very effective work around loss and its impact on clients' thinking both individually and systemically.

The following points are important to bear in mind:

- Be clear about the focus of the work and the fact that it will be time limited.

- Raise any countertransference issues and feelings in supervision. Also be aware of any transcultural aspects to the work.

- Be mindful of the last session as an ending and try to get a sense of how the client feels it has helped (or not) so that aspects of the work can be developed by other professionals.

Key points from this chapter

- Supervision is essential for any work where there is a significant amount of loss and bereavement involved. The impact of working in settings where there is regular exposure to grief should be acknowledged in a safe supervision relationship and care shown to staff who have experienced their own loss and bereavement currently or in the recent past.

- For trainees, loss and bereavement may not be the most apparent aspect of learning disabilities work but it is more common than may be first thought.

11

Working with
Terminal Illnesses

Introduction

Since the late 1970s standards of care for people with learning disabilities have improved and society's attitudes towards ill health have also changed considerably. The conditions that used to make people with learning disabilities vulnerable to a shortened lifespan have in recent times had more research and there is a greater awareness and visibility of clients with disabilities.

Standards of health care and access to specialist and mainstream health services have contributed to better care. The development of services that can advocate for better health care and focus on access have led to a significant change in life expectancy for clients.

However, this has led to an increase in people with learning disabilities presenting at general practitioners (GPs) with long-term health conditions, including serious conditions such as cardiovascular disease, stroke and cancer. It has been estimated that currently about one in ten people with learning disabilities will die from cancer and will require palliative (end of life) care (Cooke 1997). This raises all kinds of issues around joint working, ensuring standards of care across services, communication and how to approach end of life care with this client group.

Another important factor in this work is the way that it may affect others who have close relationships with those affected. As practitioners, the area of terminal illness can evoke strong feelings and these have to be managed too through supervision.

Why terminal illness is a difficult area

For many people the whole area of terminal illness is a painful one. As a society we are still not good at dealing with our fear of death and the reality of it. People with learning disabilities unfortunately will have been more exposed to it than most. A number of learning disabilities result from trauma at birth, or initiating health conditions such as epilepsy.

Having survived a number of threats to one's life, facing a terminal illness can be tragic for both the individual and their family. Terminal illness confronts us with many aspects of the human condition and the meaning of life. When this includes having to reflect on the nature and meaning of having a disability this can make such thinking harder. As one parent said:

> We spent years looking after him, giving him the best opportunities, fighting for his rights at different stages. I never thought he would go before me with this illness. (Personal communication)

It can also be a difficult area for carers who may have chosen to go into this area of work, knowing that there is a higher incidence of premature death. Having formed a meaningful relationship with clients often over many years, it can be hard to be witness to their illness. Sufficient time is rarely given to reflective thinking in staff teams or in supervision as to the impact of terminal illnesses facing clients and it is important to do so especially at times of difficulty.

Delays in diagnosis

A number of factors mean that people with learning disabilities are less likely to get an early diagnosis of a serious illness. Some medical conditions are more visible than others and happen suddenly, such as stroke, heart attack and epilepsy, whereas others – such as heart disease, cancer and dementia – may be in their early stages without being noticed. This is true of the general population but is accentuated in learning disabilities.

The specific difficulty for people with learning disabilities is that notifying carers or medical professionals of any symptoms can be complicated by difficulties in communication and other factors. Delaying any presentation for treatment can ultimately mean that any treatment comes too little, too late, and will be more distressing to the client.

It is important to be honest with people about their bodies and of being able to locate any symptoms, regions of pain or observable changes and not be afraid to do so. Clients may be reluctant to do so for the following reasons:

- Fearing the consequences of telling someone especially if it leads to nothing being found. This may be reinforced by older parents who 'don't want to make a fuss' or for older parents who do not feel confident within the UK system of health care or may not understand it.

- Being unable to put into words the feeling or sensation that is different and holding a fear of what it might be.

- Believing that their pain is caused by something that they have done wrong.

Assumptions made by others

It is common for assumptions to be made about people with learning disabilities' health. If a client has behavioural problems, or is always seeking attention, this can desensitize people to them. Actions can be put down to learned behaviour and seen as predictable. It is easy to assume that they are all right, especially with people who have less communication or who are more passive and don't change much from month to month. Unless there is any major mood change, or visible illness, people's health needs can become routine and changes may not be noticed until an illness has progressed to a critical stage.

National Strategy for End of Life Care 2008

In the UK the National Strategy for End of Life Care came about in order to give some consistency to how services are provided and managed for people approaching the end of their lives (Department of Health 2008). It is relevant to anyone who is involved with end of life care and affects the way that services are provided in hospices, hospitals and care homes as well as for primary care trusts providing care for people in the community.

The UK National End of Life Care pathway sets out six clear steps or stages to be followed that affects everyone facing end of life. These steps are the same for everyone. There are no differences for people with learning disabilities. However, the way that the patient would be involved in their own planning and individual decisions within each step may alter how it is presented. All stages involve cooperation between relevant agencies.

The National Council for Palliative Care define end of life care as 'the active holistic care of patients with advanced progressive illness' (National Council for Palliative Care 2009).

The six steps outlined in the End of Life Care pathway are as follows:

1. Discussions as the end of life approaches.

2. Assessment care planning and review.

3. Coordination of care for individual patients.

4. Delivery of high-quality services in different settings.

5. Care in the last days of life.

6. Care after death.

There is an expectation that support should be provided for carers and families as well as information for patients and families. Spiritual care is seen as being an essential component of the support that should be available.

The concept of death

To many people who have not experienced a bereavement or loss, the concept of death and dying can assume a rather abstract character. It can be an experience that is associated with later years rather than something that is faced from a young age. Having a learning disability can expose someone to death a lot earlier. The incidence of death at special schools and adult day centres confirms the fact that there is a greater vulnerability to people with learning disabilities due to degenerative and physical conditions.

Being around such experiences can mean that there is a greater acceptance of mortality. However, having greater exposure to death as a professional can be hard to manage, especially if we have invested a lot in the individual's care and have known them for a long time. One occupational therapist said:

> I felt a lot of sadness that he had died especially after we had done so much work together over the years getting him resettled in his new home. I had known him years ago when he lived in hospital and

we did lots of work, first when he moved back into the community and then into his new home. He talked about how he wanted to be there for the next 15 years and then last year he got ill and died. (Personal communication)

Such experiences connect to our own sense of why we do what we do and it can be hard yet satisfying to know that working with someone has improved their quality of life and that we had a part in making that change happen. For many people this touches upon their values and beliefs and it is important to touch upon these when these experiences occur. As professionals the ethical considerations of practice are often referred to in relation to good practice but less so about how our personal ethics and beliefs inform what we do.

Clients who we work with also have to find their own explanations around death and knowing that someone they love and care for has only a limited amount of time left. It is helpful in these situations if the person with learning disabilities is aware of this to have a conversation with their family about how they can prepare for an ending so that there is a greater involvement in the process. Often the subject is avoided directly but referred to obliquely.

Michael Jacobs (2005) summarizes this well when he states that:

> in a society where death is so often institutionalized and locked away, facing the dying and facing death is not surprisingly overloaded with fantasies of the most negative kind. Even direct experience of another's death (and that is not as common as it once was) cannot adequately prepare a person for his or her own since it is impossible to conceptualize it. (Jacobs 2005, p.97)

In assessing someone's knowledge of death and dying it is usually possible to get an idea of the beliefs that clients hold by asking them what they think happens after someone dies and what they believe happens to the deceased person.

Knowledge of what a terminal illness is

The way we construct time is mainly responsible for our managing perspective on events and how we frame events and phases of our life. Knowing that we have a fixed time period in which to complete a piece of work can concentrate the mind and enable us to do it quicker. When people are given a terminal diagnosis, it is often said that having a positive frame of mind can extend life and its quality.

In learning disabilities, there is often a more subliminal message going on: from birth there is often an expectation of shorter life yet they may not be aware of this. These issues are often brushed under the carpet and consequently kept from clients. Society's taboos around death and talking openly around it adds to this repression.

When people with learning disabilities have a terminal diagnosis, they either may not be told or may not be capable of understanding this. Many people believe that in not being told of the certainty of death they will survive for longer. However, some people will have experienced near death experiences at the start of their lives and through the course of treatment or health crises such as epilepsy.

Alternatively, in the past, a terminal diagnosis meant that people with learning disabilities were 'written off' and allowed to die earlier. Their own consent (or not being able to consent) to treatment may have meant that they were treated or allowed to die earlier for the sake of the carers. Nowadays there are clear protocols about end of life care and consent that ensure better treatment.

Maintaining identity

In her book *On Death and Dying* Elisabeth Kübler-Ross (1970) stated that:

> Dying becomes lonely and impersonal because the patient is often taken out of his familiar environment and rushed to an emergency ward. ...It would take so little to remember that the sick person too has feelings, wishes, and opinions and has – most important of all – the right to be heard. (Kübler-Ross 1970, p.7)

Mainly due to practitioners such as Kübler-Ross and the promoters of the hospice movements in the UK and in other countries, the above scenarios are now, on the whole, avoided and the managing of terminal illness has developed around maximizing the quality of life and care and also being aware of creating the right environment and promoting choices that people can make in preparation for the end of life.

Maintaining identity is so important at this stage as a way of retaining who we are and what defines our life as it has been. Our sense of ourselves – our ego – basically remains intact throughout the course of our life and can withstand many stresses. The process of reviewing life often begins by affirming identity. Many people with learning disabilities are able to achieve this by having photos of themselves at different stages of life, doing 'life book' exercises (see Chapter 8) and talking to family, friends and staff who visit. This all helps the reflective process of thinking around 'Who am I?' and 'What is my life about?'

When working with clients around their knowledge of their illness, it is important to maintain a positive sense of identity. Being in a hospital or hospice or having to spend more time at home means that people lose contact with friends and wider family.

Specific issues for adults with learning disabilities facing end of life illness

Planning

In thinking about the reality of an end of life diagnosis, it really depends on family members and the advice of medical staff as to what should be disclosed. A more helpful approach is to concentrate on the things that people want to do while they still have enough strength and health. Sometimes people will ask to go to a favourite place for a day out and this will be possible. One staff member at a palliative care unit where a patient with learning disabilities was staying said:

> We decided to take J out today because it was a sunny day and his breathing was good. However, we knew that in two months time, it might not have been possible so we had to make the most of now. (Personal communication)

Helping people to think of the things that they would like to do is all part of creating a sense of fulfilment at this stage. Planning for it makes it happen and helps to achieve another part of the 'unfinished business' that many people like to complete.

Loneliness

It is difficult to get the right balance when people with learning disabilities are facing end of life. Some relatives may believe that they need to stay with people to minimize the risk that they will become scared or anxious on their own. However, part of the task of coming towards the end of life when you are facing this may be to have some time to reflect, be still and have time on your own. It is difficult to get the right balance but the most important thing is to ask the person concerned if they want some company. For people who have less language, they will communicate this in other ways.

Lack of role models

Part of the difficulty when facing terminal illness is feeling that you are the only one in your situation. Such illness can be isolating. It is important to get some idea of the client's understanding of their illness and how it affects them, such as the changes that they notice. Sometimes there are examples of illness played out in storylines in soap operas that can be a reference point for people, but these are rare.

It can be helpful to think about previous people in the client's life who became ill and did not recover. However, the reality is that such illness is made more difficult for clients because of the lack of comparative experience from other people.

Celebrity deaths sometimes give a role model, such as reality TV star Jade Goody, and these examples can be helpful in helping the person with learning disabilities to understand that unexpected death can happen at times without much warning. A recent health study concluded that men have a statistically much higher risk of developing health problems as well and that they should be encouraged to take account of lifestyle and health risks.

Consent to treatment

The issue of consent around testing and treatment is one that affects people with learning disabilities across the board. Consent to testing and treatment inevitably involves ethical questions about when and whether it is right to administer tests and treatment to people who cannot consent, whereas many tests are essential in being able to assess someone's current health risk factors in the future and current treatment if any early signs of disease have been found.

Clinicians, carers and families are often anxious about these areas, especially if there are any concerns about consenting to treatment. However, consent is required for treatment and is politically a sensitive area for many people. No one can consent on behalf of an adult who is not competent to give consent such as in the cases of people with more severe learning disabilities.

Where there is any doubt, the situations are resolved by holding a meeting of medical and psychology professionals to discuss what is in the best interests of the person concerned. MENCAP, in considering the rights of people with learning disabilities facing medical interventions, has also been a major contributor since the late 1980s to the issue of people's rights and the importance of consent to treatment and having treatments explained to enable understanding.

These areas may come into sharper focus when someone has an illness from which they are unlikely to recover. However, it is at these times when everyone involved with an individual's physical and psychological health have to work together for the client's best interests and health.

The following example (from some years ago) shows how easy it is for health needs to be neglected and what can occur in terms of greater health needs when people's needs become more complex.

Case study: Lydia

Lydia was a 61-year-old woman with autism and echolalia who had recently been saying that she felt 'ill'. She lived in a residential home with five others and had always had a reputation for being a bit vulnerable in terms of her health. Instead of taking her needs seriously, staff often thought that she was prone to anxiety. A number of years beforehand her family had similarly not taken her health needs seriously; she had developed complications which then necessitated surgery as she had left things too long.

Years before she had expressed her fears by biting herself and attempting to bite others, and the whole process of engaging with health professionals was fraught with problems. This had been very distressing for her and she subsequently developed a health anxiety about going to see her doctor. No one at the time really did much reflective thinking about how her behaviour was mainly about anxiety and she was left with a reputation as being 'difficult'.

As a result of this Lydia did not go to see the doctor often and either would refuse to go or would create a lot of stress around her so that sometimes she would have to go home before she had been in to the surgery. When eventually a doctor came to see her, he advised that she go into hospital to have some tests as 'something was not right'.

A best interests meeting was called and recommendations were made for the treatment to be much more focused around her engagement and being supportive. Surgery was planned and the process of admission went well. Lydia had a communication board with Makaton symbols that helped her to communicate her needs more easily when in hospital. Despite the fact that she 'hated' hospitals, this visit was 'better' she said because the 'staff' were nice to her.

Sadly within a couple of years Lydia died from cancer that was detected following on from the tests. In that time, however, having overcome her fears she had been able to have greater support from the staff and some guidelines were drawn up about with her about how she liked to be treated by other people when she went to appointments and when she was in hospital. She also had an advocate from a local organization to help her communicate her needs.

The following points can be made from this case example:

- Clients can have traumatic memories of past medical interventions that prevent them from engaging well with health professionals.

- It is important not to ignore individuals' reporting of pain or health concerns and to take these seriously.

- Careful planning and sensitive working with people to acknowledge and address some of their fears can avoid situations becoming more difficult.

- Creating a calm consistent approach to care is particularly helpful to clients with behavioural difficulties and limited expressive language.

Explaining a terminal diagnosis

It is important at the start of any explanation of a serious health condition that the person concerned is told the truth. When answering questions, professionals should always be honest and avoid euphemisms; clear and unambiguous language should be used at all times. It is important not to avoid the truth as clients may subsequently feel that they have been let down by others and this can impede their acceptance of the condition.

Having explained the prognosis it is important to give someone hope while giving people time to reflect with family and friends about the future. The support of family and friends is crucial at this time. It may also be useful at some later stage (for example of a therapeutic relationship) for clients to share their fears about death and what they think may happen including any ideas of what happens after the end. People may have had latent fears about death for some time that have not been explored and if they wish they can find it helpful to gain reassurance from the staff caring for them.

Keeping in contact with family and friends is very important as they are a form of continuity. It can be reassuring when a palliative care team become involved as their approach can seem less medical and more holistic, thinking of the wider needs of the person concerned. If clients move to a hospice, this is another change but one that brings a different more healing environment.

Palliative care

In 1990, the World Health Organization defined palliative care as 'the active total care of patients whose disease is not responsive to curative treatment; the goal of palliative care is achievement of the best quality of life for patients and their families' (WHO 1990).

Generally the term palliative care seems to have become much more commonly used to describe the type of treatment available to patients where there is no 'cure' as such. This may have a certain resonance for parents of learning disabled children born some years ago when they were told that there was little or no hope for their young child and no 'cure' as such. Attitudes have thankfully changed since then, yet we often hope for cures for physical illnesses that are not as yet available. Attitudes to dying are also changing, and there is often a stated aim of helping someone to have a 'good death' where time is afforded to planning and acting on what the client's wishes are.

Monitoring pain is another significant aspect of the work that medical staff do and it is important to be aware of how individuals concerned communicate pain and what can be done to alleviate it.

The World Health Organization has taken an international role in the policies that have influenced national thinking across the world. The 2010 Healthy People initiative (US Department of Health and Human Services 2000) is the most recent focusing on prevention but follows on from the 1990 Cancer Pain initiative (WHO 1990). These are all relevant and will affect the way that anyone (including those with learning disabilities) will be treated.

Health education

Following an individual's death from a terminal illness, it is important to consider how much health education those left behind are receiving. Promoting good accurate health education – from dental hygiene, healthy eating and lifestyle to regular health screenings for women and men – is essential to give other people with learning disabilities the feeling that they are being looked after as much as possible, that their health is important and that they are getting all the information backed up by good health advice appointments where necessary to limit the risks to their own health.

Again communication is important and making changes to people's lifestyle and routine to promote good health cannot be imposed on people without their agreement.

Staff, parents and carers should be as informed as possible about maintaining health and well-being: being mindful of risks is an important part of the legacy of terminal illness. Being seen to do this and promote the health of others can be a reassuring factor for people we care for. It can also be a factor in 'preventable death', where having access to information can make further illness less likely to go unnoticed.

Supporting people with learning disabilities who have terminally ill relatives and friends

When supporting a client who has a terminally ill relative, it is important to be sensitive to other family members or friends who are facing a loss. Identify what needs to be done on behalf of the client you are supporting and communicate this to significant family members.

Many services have policies around managing these situations. Hospices invariably have good systems in place that not only facilitate the end of life for individuals but also offer ongoing support to relatives after a death. This is part of the End of Life Care strategy and website information is listed at the end of this book.

In addition, the following points are helpful if you are the main carer supporting someone with learning disabilities:

- Identify other people who can also have a supportive role so that if you are not working then you are not worrying about leaving the client without support. Also identify the wider support around accountability (e.g. service managers).

- Be as clear as possible about your role and ensure that family members, hospital staff and hospice staff are clear about your role. They will also be able to help think about any specific needs that the person with learning disabilities concerned may have.

- Be as honest as you feel you can be but also communicate in a way that will not present people with undue or extra anxieties.

- Be supportive and facilitate visits to the person who is ill if both wish that to happen.

- Phone ahead prior to a visit so that the individual avoids stressful situations. Have the name of a member of staff who is your main contact.

- Be clear in communicating what is happening and check that the person you are supporting understands what is happening.

- Get support for yourself as this can be emotionally demanding. Good supportive supervision is essential.

Key points from this chapter

- If you are a parent or carer be mindful of the fact that people with learning disabilities are just as much at risk of chronic health conditions and terminal illness as anyone else. It is essential that we are watchful for any symptoms that may be indicative of illness and pain as well as being mindful of family history of illness.

- It is important that religious and cultural observations are respected and that individuals are supported in this.

- It is vital that the End of Life Care plans (or equivalent in other countries) are put in place so that there is consistency and an acceptance of a staged supportive process. This will help individuals and their families (or people with learning disabilities who have partners or family members facing end of life) to feel more secure and psychologically held by services.

12

Remembering and Anniversaries

Introduction

The role of anniversaries and the importance of holding memories of someone who has died is a key part of psychologically internalizing the loss. Anniversaries form an important part of the bereavement process by helping people to reflect on the way that they have managed during the time past. It can also highlight how someone has moved on since the loss. Some people find that the time around an anniversary can lead to a slight step back as memories can upset us and temporarily bring back some of the grief.

With clients who have learning disabilities the role that anniversaries play can be potentially more difficult. There is less space to do this reflection. Dates and times can be easily overlooked and an anniversary may pass without the bereaved person having had it acknowledged. If someone has had to move home following bereavement, they may hold their memories alone, particularly if no one knew them where they used to live. Feeling alone at times like this can accentuate the sadness.

It is common for people with learning disabilities who have been bereaved and who are facing the first anniversary of this to focus on it, especially if they have been 'helpfully' reminded of it by others. This can be done with the best of intentions but can complicate the individual's own way of managing.

Sometimes losses can be related: for some people with learning disabilities the death of a parent, for example, may have been preceded by that parent having a period of illness or going into hospital. The date of a death may be less important to them than the date of the funeral or when they moved. Losses can be associated with specific events or time of the year. They can also be markers of time that can be significant and helpful in the process of helping people move on.

Functions of remembering

Remembering or recalling a person or a time to do with bereavement is important to us as it helps to keep the memory of a deceased person alive. It is also important with clients who have learning disabilities to be able to do this in a way that is helpful and not bringing back distress unnecessarily.

It can be hard to know what to do if an anniversary is approaching, especially if the individual has found the grieving process to be difficult. There can be the dilemma of whether to mention it or to minimize it for fear of making the situation worse. Yet not acknowledging it can feel as if it is negating the person's experience. Past events such as bereavements and losses can continue to have a major impact on people in their present lives. Anniversaries can become the focus for this.

In considering marking an anniversary the following points should be considered:

- Why is the anniversary significant?
- Who has initiated this?
- Who is the person being helped?
- What impact is the marking of the anniversary going to have on the individual concerned?
- Is it clear whether the individual has psychologically located the loss in a safe place for them so that they can cope with thinking about it?

For any grieving individual, there is a fundamental negotiation required around where and how to place the memory of the deceased person. The reality is that when someone is no longer there, the active relationship ceases. However, we can often find ourselves mulling over events from the past and wishing that things were different. It is our need to make sense of the past and the role that we had in relation to the person who is no longer here. Current feelings about past relationships can be ambivalent and difficult to correct or alter. This can be very confusing for people with learning disabilities who have histori-cally experienced that information is kept from them on the premise that it is 'for their own good' or 'it may upset them'.

It is common to idealize someone after they have died, perhaps as a way of not wanting to think about the aspects of their personality, actions or behaviour that we did not like. Some people instinctively block out or don't talk about unpleasant memories of conflict or past abuses through a feeling of loyalty. How people tell their life stories is inevitably going to be biased according to their experience of events. To complicate things further, particularly in residential services or day services, other people may have vastly different opinions and experi-ences of the deceased friend or relative. It is common for staff members and professionals to know confidential information relating to the his-tory of the person being cared for that can be extremely sensitive. The way that this is held in a safe way depends on the way that services react and the way that confidentiality policies are implemented.

In taking or assimilating information about a client's history, it is always important to attain relevant facts but not to be surprised if, subsequent to bereavement, clients disclose information that might have been suspected but never proved.

Recalling the past

Grief work inevitably involves the recall of past memories. This has to be done with care, particularly if it has the potential to awaken past traumatic memories. The impact of traumatic events that may or may not have been uncovered in an individual's past can lie unnoticed for many years. Care has to be taken in recalling the past to be mindful of this and making onward referral to specialist services if necessary.

In general bereavement work, clients will have individual memo-ries and it can be helpful and comforting to recall these. Anniversaries can bring back grief and it is important that people with learning dis-abilities have access to someone to talk to about this if they wish.

Recognizing attachments

A task that is often cited in grief work is being able to begin to detach or separate from the deceased person. This is a psychological as well as a literal process. In recognizing the impact and physical reality of bereavement, it is necessary to know that the deceased person is not coming back. This can be hard, especially if there has been a history of ambivalent attachments where contact has been difficult. It can often be that early maternal bonding with infants can be disrupted for many reasons. Older people with learning disabilities, in particular, may have had difficult past experiences of being physically or psychologically abandoned.

Remembering in such circumstances can be complicated by continued ambivalent feelings that complicate the grief process, especially if the bereavement has been of a relative who did not seem to care.

In his 1913 essay 'Totem and Taboo' Freud refers to the way that attachments have to be relocated in terms of the way that we remember others: 'Mourning has quite a precise psychical task to perform: its function is to detach the survivor's hopes and memories from the dead' (p.65). This can be complex for people with learning disabilities, especially if they had a very close or a very distant relationship with the people in their life. The ability to remember is therefore compromised as it can take a long time to reach a balanced view of the deceased person.

Problems with remembering

Grieving is an expected psychological response to significant bereavement and subsequent losses. People with learning disabilities may have greater difficulty in remembering facts and circumstances around their loss for a number of reasons.

First, the impact of grief and the subsequent change that can happen following it may have distracted or shielded the individual from the actual events around the time of bereavement. It is not uncommon for many grieving individuals to go through bereavement in a 'haze of shock and grief'. Remembering particular facts and events can be hard in the face of grief. It is important to refer on to specialist services if there appears to be distress around this over a long period of time.

Second, it is possible that some confusion can set in after bereavement when recalling a series of events, especially as learning disabled clients have less influence in how such events are managed. It is also recognized that memory lapses are a common feature of behavioural and emotional change following a personal bereavement.

Third, people with learning disabilities may not have had much direct day-to-day contact with the recently deceased person, especially if they were an elderly relative who needed extra care. Physical distance can be a factor, especially if visiting is limited or if visits were deemed to be particularly upsetting for either party. Due to the nature of learning disabilities, cognitive function can be affected and so this can also affect what is retained and an increased likelihood of confusion and subsequent distress.

Marking an anniversary of a death can be very helpful in acknowledging change and progress. However, the points above may have some bearing on how helpful this is. Involving people with learning disabilities as much as possible with the thinking about how they may want to mark a first anniversary may be important but it is equally important to choose not to dwell on it if the client has not initiated this.

Aids to memory

Many people following bereavement find it important to keep personal mementoes and items that can remind them of the deceased person. These have to be regarded as being important and a link to the person who has died. Unfortunately for people with learning disabilities, they may have less choice about what is kept and they are often left out of the process of folding up a house where their parents lived. Surviving relatives should bear this in mind as the personal items that were important to the deceased person may have an unexpected emotional resonance for clients and the items may be lost in the process of sorting things out.

Photographs can be particularly helpful, especially if they feature the deceased person with the client. Early photos can helpfully demonstrate the relationship in a positive way. It is also vital that if a bereavement necessitates a move that the personal mementos are constant and are taken care of by the client themselves. Life books are another way that information is retained and carried forward for many people and can become a focus for accessing past memories. These are discussed in Chapter 8.

Holding memories of a past event or place with the help of photographs, DVD recordings and other items can be an essential way of facilitating the grief process. However, care has to be taken that exposure to memories is done in a way that helps and enables clients.

Sometimes, prior to an anniversary or on the actual day, a bereaved person can feel unwell with stomach pains or headaches. Physical manifestations of grief are common yet may be hard to explain by someone experiencing them.

When remembering is not helpful

Sometimes remembering is not helpful and can take people back to memories that they thought they had dealt with. Examples of this follow.

When a client has moved on

If a client has put a routine back in their lives that they are well established in, it can be an unwelcome disruption to actively mark the anniversary of a death.

If it reawakens memories that have previously been addressed in therapy

Therapeutic interventions, notably counselling, but also art or drama work can be helpful in addressing grief reactions. However, if interventions are ended at the wrong stage of therapy, clients can be without support when they need it most. Having access to reassurance or support around the time of anniversaries can be very helpful if clients regress in their grief.

When it is forced

It can be very unhelpful to clients to be actively encouraged to revisit places because it is the right thing to do. It is important to bear the client's needs in mind and not impose other agendas that are not part of what they want to do. Pressure to do so can be destructive and unwanted. There is no right way to mark anniversaries and it can be unnecessary.

If a client is 'stuck'

It can be inappropriate to encourage someone to remember if they are not ready to so. Sometimes people need some time to work out for themselves how they can manage their grief and this can involve not knowing what to do.

When grief has no end point

Often a funeral and the gathering afterwards can be the formal end point to 'official' grieving. It is helpful to mark a stage in the mourning process and it should be seen as a significant event prior to resuming some kind of familiar routine. If this is not done, people with learning disabilities can be left a bit confused about when the grieving ends. 'Moving on' at an appropriate time can be an essential part of containing grief.

If a client has conflicting messages from those around them

It is often the case that people are exposed to different attitudes to grief and mourning, particularly within staff teams. If this leads to conflicting messages from others about the importance or not of remembering, then clients may fear not getting support or approval for how they wish to mourn.

Managing unpleasant memories

It can be hard to be reminded of unpleasant and often traumatic memories following bereavement. Feelings of grief can be complicated by hidden anger and a desire to forget both the past and the people associated with experiences that formed these memories. It is sometimes only the death of someone that allows people to speak freely, yet this can also be confused by feelings of guilt.

If someone with learning disabilities begins to talk about unpleasant or traumatic memories or shows behavioural change such as self-harm following the death of someone, obviously what they say must be taken seriously. This should always involve onward referral to other services, but if it is following the bereavement of someone known to the client who initiated events that left the memories, it could be too late to effect any change. The focus has to be on ensuring the current physical and psychological safety of the client and on a day-to-day level providing security and care so that they have a safe place within which to talk and get support.

At the time of an anniversary, some of these memories may be reactivated. It is important to be mindful of new reactions or disclosures. Any unpleasant memories that are triggered by a specific date are less likely but still have to be taken seriously.

Unwelcome reminding

A common experience is that of a surviving parent wishing to mark the anniversary of the death of the other parent by visiting a graveside or other place of significance with their adult son or daughter. While this may be helpful for the parent, it can be difficult for the son or daughter as it brings back memories of the unhappy time, and it may not be helpful for the person with the learning disabilities themselves. They may do it out of a sense of loyalty to their remaining parent or family member, but not actually want to take part in that way as it will trigger unhappy memories.

At such times it is important to consider the function of memory when attempting to mark an anniversary, such as who is initiating the memories and the purpose of doing it. Where possible these kind of activities should be done only if there is consent from the individual and that they realize that it may bring back some upset.

Overall, however, one point remains crucial: the involvement of bereaved clients with the process of mourning will enable them to have a better outcome in resolving grief over the longer term. Having less direct involvement results in less 'ownership' of the process and a higher degree of anxiety overall. Developing this in line with choice also enables clients to have a sense of control over what they become involved with and what they choose to avoid.

Loss felt by a centre or home

When someone who has lived in a care home or residential setting dies, the way in which they are remembered can be different. Set policies are usually in place to facilitate this, but there is often little scope for further reflection at times of anniversaries. This can, of course, be dictated by the size of the home, the length of service of existing staff, the range of disabilities and communication of people within a home and the ethos of the organization that manages it.

It is important to recognize individual relationships and friendships that are set up within homes and centres. Giving time to talk about bereavement and memories that people have of former residents can give existing residents some reassurance that people are not forgotten; this is particularly important in helping them to feel more secure and valued in the here and now. The continuation of routines is reassuring and provides continuity for those left behind.

Continuity

Having a sense of continuity is central to the concerns of people with learning disabilities who are left behind after bereavement. A major bereavement is often followed by a period of change and transition that has the potential to be disruptive. Continuity has to be considered in terms of accommodation, relationships, and a sense of identity.

As a result of the changes above, bereavement can be a long process. Having a learning disability can disrupt the continuity of mourning by having other life changes in the course of it. Bereavement can leave people feeling disconnected at times and disability can add to a greater sense of isolation. Having continuity can help this and promote the process of remembering through maintaining supportive relationships with family members, support staff and friends.

Many people with learning disabilities share common memories having been to the same school, day centre or social clubs. Parents and families often know of each other through familiar networks and if there is a sense of community in the area served by local services.

Having local services based around cultural and/or social events can foster a sense of community that helps the process of remembering and makes it less likely that people lose their own sense of history and identity. This is often successful when there is a developed voluntary sector.

For people with learning disabilities, moving to live with a brother or sister following the death of a parent can be difficult if they have little or no connection with the local area. Preparation should be done in advance, ideally in thinking within a family about how to smooth the transition by having visits to local resources. It can also be an issue for clients who may have been placed in other areas that can cater for their specific needs and who then have to move back due to funding cutbacks.

Anniversaries can be helpful points at which to build a perspective on the loss that someone has experienced. Typically this can be done with reference to cultural, religious or spiritual needs to help with the development of meaning and perspective about what has happened. The search for meaning following a bereavement or loss – 'Why has this happened to me?' – can be a focus for self-learning and reflecting on that with clients at an appropriate time can be very healing for them.

Problems with anniversaries

One of the main difficulties when people with learning disabilities come to remember an anniversary or event that was significant in terms of bereavement and loss is that life will have moved on in the intervening time. They may have moved to a different area themselves, and going back to see a former house can be difficult if it reminds them of painful memories. Family homes are often sold and have new owners or new tenants living there, neighbourhoods change and take on a different atmosphere. The people who might have known the person in the past may have moved or died themselves, and so the connection with the individual is lost.

It can be difficult to explain this if you are in the position of helping someone with their memories. It is common for people to get stuck in a cycle of feeling sad because things have changed. However, it is part of the reality for clients in this position just as it is for anyone experiencing bereavement: change is inevitable and anticipating it can at least prepare for the reality of this.

Doubts about memory and relationships

After some time the initial shock of bereavement can lessen, and grief can seem to fade as new routines become established and new relationships are formed. This can be a relief for people supporting clients with learning disabilities. It appears that things are beginning to move on, as people feel less need to talk about their loss and adapt to a new set of circumstances.

Over time, this can give rise to doubts about past relationships. Older clients may forget details of someone they used to know and it can at times be distressing for the bereavement process if there are gaps missing in knowledge and in memory. This can lead to further confusion about what actually happened at key points in someone's history.

As staff move on, the sense of connection with a deceased person can also seem less. Staff who have supported clients who are experiencing grief can play a vital role that newer staff cannot do if they didn't know the person's family or past friends.

One way that this can be helped is by reminiscence work where photos and other visual memories can be shared as a gradual way of getting to know someone's history. There is an inherent risk in this, especially if the new person also leaves within a short space of time. Having a specific number of sessions for reminiscence work in a counselling or psychotherapy intervention can be a way of working around this.

Wherever possible the person's emotional experience of the events that they remember should be reflected and believed as this holds the key to good reminiscence work and makes it more effective in enabling clients to make meaningful connections. Putting memories and experiences into a meaningful perspective is a crucial part of finding a sense of hope eventually and of retaining a sense of self as the bereavement process unfolds.

Creating a focus

Creating a focus for memories can help people to feel that there has been a sense of containment in remembering and acknowledging anniversaries. Creating a memorial following a death, some time after a funeral, can be another step in moving on in remembering. Some people may find comfort in attending religious or other community events that help them to focus their thoughts.

However, care should be taken to focus on memories that are going to help. Creating a focus to remember that takes people to a place that brings back unhappy memories can be distressing and unhelpful. Of course, talking with the person about what they would like to do is the most important factor here: assuming that a certain activity will help when it clearly will not is to be avoided.

If activities are planned around Christmas, Easter or other religious festivals, this should be done with care, particularly if it is the first year since bereavement. It is likely that clients will be missing the person more at these times and be more emotionally vulnerable.

Unresolved grief appearing some time after a loss

It is acknowledged that some resolution is necessary for grief to subside. For people with learning disabilities, this may be having as many opportunities to talk or act upon their emotional, physical or behavioural responses as possible. This is inevitably going to necessitate a proactive stance from those around them in enabling them to get the help that is needed. Some people do not necessarily require formalized help, but it is important to have the opportunity to do so if required.

It is important to see the significance of grief appearing at a specific time if it is delayed. The pain of grief can sometimes block out memories that have been repressed for some time. Getting them back can be a positive sign but can also necessitate further therapeutic work, especially if it leads to distress. Bereavement is not a smooth journey where events and feelings appear as if in some narrative form. Some people with learning disabilities find that memories can come back at seemingly random intervals.

Case study: John

John was a man in his early sixties who had lived with his mum until the age of 29. He had a moderate learning disability and had always been independent, moving into a supported house for eight years. At the age of 38, having had a relationship with another service user, Carol, for just over five years, they decided to get married and moved in to a flat with minimal support.

After 18 years of marriage, Carol became ill and was diagnosed with leukaemia. By the time of diagnosis it was fairly advanced, and despite a long course of treatment she died two years later. John and Carol had been married for 20 years and now John was allocated a social worker. He was finding it hard to cope and was feeling lonely; when a place came available at a small house with three other men, he said he would like to move in there for a while.

The placement was going well until the first anniversary of Carol's death came up. John became preoccupied with thoughts about how he could remember events and wanted to be able to remember every detail that he could. He was referred for some counselling sessions and the focus became how he could mark the anniversary on his own terms. It seemed important for him to be able to give himself permission not to remember absolutely every detail. Everyone else was becoming concerned that he had become more anxious although it was understood that the anniversary was significant.

John commented that his friends seemed to have forgotten about the anniversary and he felt hurt by this, despite everyone remembering them as a couple. In one meeting with his key worker he became very angry and said that he was fed up that no one remembered and that all the staff were either 'telling him what he should do' or 'not helping'.

The counselling sessions helped him to think about what he wanted and how he could do what he wanted in the way that he wanted. It helped that the sessions were independent of the services that he used. In thinking about the actual day, John decided to go to a local place where they had visited regularly when they had met and to lay some flowers in a favourite place for both of them.

John spent time planning how he would spend the day of the anniversary and what he would do at different points in the day. Anticipating the feelings he expected to feel seemed to help him to prepare for the fact it would be difficult but having practised some stress management techniques, John said that he thought he would be all right. Involving his key worker by telling her of the plans meant that the key worker could support him yet also not worry about how he would be on the day.

One of the main benefits of John doing this was that he was able to take ownership of his own grief and remembering. One of the functions of anniversaries is to keep memories alive and it can be very helpful to do something to mark them, especially after one year.

Seasons and festivals

Significant factors affecting grief after one year can be the weather and annual events. People often associate events with specific dates and times of the year and these can evoke pleasant or unwelcome thoughts and associations. Bereavement around the time of significant festivals such as Christmas, Ramadan or Diwali can be difficult as the person grieving may associate the loss with these events. The weather or season can be equally evocative. Having a learning disability may make a specific date harder to recall but a particular season can bring back memories recalled by the quality of the light or by the weather or temperature.

Voices, accents, smells and sounds

Older clients who have been in the care system for a long time often have memories of long-term institutions where they have lived for many years. The old hospitals that closed in the 1970s and 1980s were often located outside of town centres and for people who lived there formed a major part of their earlier lives. The particular smells and sounds associated with these institutions and the routines established may be consigned to history, but it is important to recognize when triggers may return, maybe by someone's accent, tone of voice or manner in which they speak. Being mindful of these triggers is about being mindful of clients' personal histories.

Although people's lives have changed considerably since then, these clients may be the last people to remember a hospital that held ambivalent feelings and memories for them. It represented a loss of the past and those around them. Some of these memories can be brought back in the way that 'endings' are managed when staff leave or other clients die.

When staff who have had a long connection with clients leave, it is inevitable that feelings of loss will be there. There may be a sense of resentment from some clients or guilt from longstanding staff that they have their retirement to look forward to while the people they have cared for are still in a position of comparative dependency.

Dementia

Clients who experience a bereavement when a parent dies following progressive dementia may have seen their loved one decline in terms of function and their own memory. This can be particularly distressing for clients who have struggled to understand what dementia is as well as how and why it happens. Clients may well have known grandparents or fellow service residents who lived with dementia for some years.

In terms of remembering, it is usual after about a year for memories of the deceased person to have recovered so that there can be pleasant memories about how the person was in former times. In this way remembering can be a healing way of reclaiming the memory of someone who was in effect lost to the client before they passed away.

Case study: Rachel

Rachel had lived with her mum until she was 41. She had a moderate learning disability and had a job working part time in a local shop while her mum stayed at home. Over time Rachel had noticed that her mum had changed and that she wasn't able to do some of the things that she had been able to do, such as washing herself and keeping the house clean. She tended to compensate and said to herself that this was what happened when parents got older.

When she came back from work one afternoon, Rachel found the front door open and her mum walking outside in a disorientated state. She was surprised by this but thought it was 'something that older people did'. She took her mum back inside and thought nothing more of it. However, a few other changes and incidents happened over time that Rachel thought were either worrying or her mum being 'silly'. Her mum kept on forgetting things, including her birthday, which Rachel was upset about.

By the time her mum went looking for 'something she had lost' at 2.30 in the morning and was brought back by the police, Rachel was very unhappy and told the police that she needed help with her mum because her mum hadn't been able to help her for a long time now and she was worried.

After her mum had been placed in residential care, Rachel's routine changed and she visited her often. However, the mum that she had known 'was no longer there' as she said. When her mum died about a year later, it took Rachel time to readjust. She found that she was living more independently and had adjusted to living on her own with a weekly visit from a support worker. The hardest part, she said to the worker, was letting go of the unhappy and confusing time when her mum had 'changed', but she was getting to a position where she could remember her mum as she was before the dementia, which made it easier for her.

Managing change

Managing change is never easy following bereavement and loss particularly in the area of learning disabilities. Change is inevitable but hard for many clients to accept as it invariably involves facing the reality of death and loss when witnessing the illness and decline of another, often a close relative, or friend with whom there is a regular intimate contact that will have altered over time. Change can be perceived as being sudden and unexpected as for many people with learning disabilities there is less chance for variety and change due to the limitations that disability imposes on them.

Change often happens without warning and so can be especially hard to manage due to its suddenness. Anniversaries can be a positive reminder for people of how they successfully managed to adapt.

It is important to have trusting people to share memories with if it is leading to distress. Being there for clients who have to manage change is essential for their successful resolution of loss and adjusting to a new situation.

A significant part of managing change in the first year following bereavement involves getting used to new routines, which can be difficult for clients with learning disabilities. If you are supporting someone to do this, the following points will be familiar to you:

- Involving clients in the thinking through of what they want to do and building in clear choices can result in them adapting more successfully.

- Allowing time to get used to a new routine and trying to avoid having to change suddenly in a way that may disorientate someone promotes its long-term effectiveness.

- Setting aside time to talk through with people about their feelings and listening to things that may be difficult can make adjustment easier. Some clients may appear to be inflexible and there may be a disruption to their behaviour for some time, but this is a way of assuming control over a situation that is essentially one that is new, unfamiliar and at times frightening. Anniversaries may bring these feelings back but they will subside again.

When to end mourning and remembering

Often there is no clear point at which mourning ends. It is common to want to avoid signifying an end to mourning as such, in case insufficient time has been given to recognize the loss. It may be hard to trust that it has in fact eased.

At the same time, it can be that without a clear closure or 'moving on', it can feel like there is no resolution and the process of mourning loses something. In fact life can feel that it just moves on of its own accord and routines become established that take over.

Establishing these new routines is essential in helping clients to have a sense of safety and security. Some clients can find this reassuring and soon fit in to new routines if they are well thought through.

It is important to remember that recalling memories can be very therapeutic for people and it is not something to be feared. Many memories are the source of affection and the focus for love that was and is still held for someone from our past. Sensitive support around memories can promote a deeper understanding of the value that someone has on our own lives. Clients are often able to reflect on this in a way that helps them rather than distresses them. Continuing activities such as social clubs that the deceased person used to take a part in can help the existing members to know that life goes on and memories are an important part of communal life. Existing networks of support continue and in many people's experience remembering is a part of their own history.

Key points from this chapter

The importance of recognizing memories following bereavement and loss cannot be underestimated. It validates the loss of the grieving individual, gives weight to the significance of enduring attachments and relationships that people with learning disabilities have, and can communicate important but often unspoken messages about loss and how it can be tolerated in a way that does not have to be hidden or the focus of internalized shame. It is possible to validate the desire and need to remember in a way that can help someone to be more comfortable with the reality of their loss and give the implicit message that this can be achieved.

If you are in this situation as a carer, the following points could be helpful when being with someone who is grieving around the process of remembering:

- Try to encourage the person to talk about their feelings and recognize that memories are part of a more positive side of grieving, although they may bring back some sadness.

- Think with the person about if they would like to do something to mark the anniversary. However, if they do not want to, then do not insist. It is likely to be helpful for some people but not for everyone.

- If you are a brother or sister who now cares for your sibling following the death of your mutual parents, remember that you will potentially find the anniversay hard yourself.

- Encourage the use of photos, DVDs and video in reminiscing about the deceased person.

- Reassure the person of their physical safety and of having managed a stressful situation well.

REFERENCES

Atkinson, D., Jackson, M. and Walmsley, J. (eds) (1997) *Forgotten Lives: Exploring the History of Learning Disability*. Kidderminster: BILD.

Blackman, N. (2003) *Loss and Learning Disability*. London: Worth.

Bond, T. (2000) *Standards and Ethics for Counselling in Action*, 2nd edn. London: Sage.

Bond, T. (2002) *Ethical Framework for Good Practice in Counselling and Psychotherapy*. Rugby: British Association for Counselling and Psychotherapy.

Carr, A. (2000) *Family Therapy: Concepts, Process and Practice*. Chichester: Wiley.

Carter, B. and McGoldrick, M. (eds) (1985) *The Changing Family Life Cycle: A Framework for Family Therapy*. New York: Gardner.

Clark, C.L. (2001) *Adult Day Services and Social Inclusion: Better Days*. London: Jessica Kingsley Publishers.

Cooke, L.B. (1997) 'Cancer and learning disability.' *Journal of Intellectual Disability Research 41*, 4, 312–316.

D'Ardenne, P. and Mahtani, A. (1989) *Transcultural Counselling in Action*. London: Sage.

Department of Health (2001a) *Consent: A Guide for People with Learning Disabilities*. London: Department of Health.

Department of Health (2001b) *Valuing People: A New Strategy for Learning Disability for the 21st Century*, Cm 5086. London: The Stationery Office.

Department of Health (2007a) *Mental Capacity Act 2005*. London: Department of Health. Available at www.opsi.gov.uk/acts/acts2005/ukpga_20050009_en_1, accessed on 24 August 2009.

Department of Health (2007b) *Mental Health Act 2007*. London: Department of Health. Available at www.opsi.gov.uk/acts/acts2007/ukpga_20070012_en_1, accessed on 24 August 2009.

Department of Health (2008) *National Strategy for End of Life Care*. London: Department of Health. Available at www.dh.gov.uk/en/Healthcare/IntegratedCare/Endoflifecare, accessed on 24 August 2009.

Emerson, E. and Hatton, C. (2004) *Estimating Future Need/Demand for Supports for Adults with Learning Disabilities in England*. Lancaster: Institute for Health Research, Lancaster University.

Foundation for People with Learning Disabilities (2007) 'Statistics on learning disabilities.' Available at www.learningdisabilities.org.uk/information/learning-disabilities-statistics/?locale=en, accessed 21 October 2009.

Freud, S. (1904) 'Freud's Psycho-Analytic Procedure.' *The Standard Edition of the Complete Psychological Works of Sigmund Freud, Volume VII*. London: Hogarth Press.

Freud, S. (1913) 'Totem and Taboo.' *The Standard Edition of The Complete Psychological Works of Sigmund Freud*. London: Hogarth Press.

Hawkins, P. and Shohet, R. (2007) *Supervision in the Helping Professions*, 3rd edn. Maidenhead: Open University Press.

Hirst, M. (2004) *Hearts and Minds: The Health Effects of Caring*. York: Social Policy Research Unit, University of York.

Hollins, S. (1995) *Managing Grief Better: People with Intellectual Disabilities*. Available at www.intellectualdisability.info/mental_phys_health/P_grief_sh.html, accessed 21 October 2009.

Hollins, S. and Esterhuyzen, A. (1997) 'Bereavement and grief in adults with learning disabilities.' *British Journal of Psychiatry 170*, June, 497–501.

Holmes, J. (1993) *John Bowlby and Attachment Theory*. London: Routledge.

Holmes, J. and Lindley, R. (1989) *The Values of Psychotherapy*. Oxford: Oxford University Press.

Horowitz, M.J., Bonanno, G.A. and Holen, A. (1993) 'Pathological grief: Diagnosis and explanation.' *Psychosomatic Medicine 55*, 3, 260–273.

Jacobs, M. (2005) *The Presenting Past*, 3rd edn. Maidenhead: Open University Press.

Kadushin, A. and Harkness, D. (2002) *Supervision in Social Work*, 4th edn. New York: Columbia University Press.

Kanner, L. (1943) 'Autistic disturbances of affective contact.' *Nervous Child 2*, 217–250.

Kerr, M.P., Richards, D. and Glover, G. (1996) 'Primary care for people with an intellectual disability – a group practice study.' *Journal of Applied Research in Intellectual Disability 9*, 4, 347–352.

Kübler-Ross, E. (1970) *On Death and Dying*. London: Tavistock.

Mattison, V. and Pistrang, N. (2000) *Saying Goodbye: When Keyworker Relationships End*. London: Free Association Books.

National Council for Palliative Care (2009) 'Palliative Care Explained.' Available at www.ncpc.org.uk/palliative_care.html, accessed 23 October 2009.

O'Brien, J. (1989) *What's Worth Working For? Leadership for Better Quality Human Services*. Available at http://thechp.syr.edu//whatsw.pdf, accessed 21 October 2009.

Oswin, M. (1991) *Am I Allowed to Cry? A Study of Bereavement among People Who Have Learning Difficulties*. London: Human Horizon.

Parkes, C.M. (1972) *Bereavement: Studies of Grief in Adult Life*. London: Penguin.

Sarafino, E. (1998) *Health Psychology: Biopsychological Interactions*, 3rd edn. New York, NY: Wiley.

Spiller, M.J. and Gratsa, A. (2004) 'Autism.' In G. Holt, A. Gratsa, N. Bouras, T. Boyce, M.J. Spiller and S. Hardy (eds) *Guide to Mental Health for Families and Carers of People with Intellectual Disabilities*. London: Jessica Kingsley Publishers.

US Department of Health and Human Services (2000) *Healthy People 2010: Understanding and Improving Health*, 3rd edn. Washington, DC: Government Printing Office.

Wilson, S. (2003) *Disabilities, Counselling and Psychotherapy: Challenges and Opportunities*. Basingstoke: Palgrave Macmillan.

Worden, J.W. (2003) *Grief Counselling and Grief Therapy: A Handbook for the Mental Health Practitioner*, 3rd edn. London: Brunner-Routledge.

World Health Organization (1980) *International Classification of Impairments, Disabilities and Handicaps*. Geneva: WHO.

World Health Organization (1990) *Cancer Pain Relief and Palliative Care*. Geneva: WHO.

FURTHER READING

Barbera, T.C., Pitch, R.J. and Howell, M.C. (1989) *Death and Dying: A Guide for Staff Serving Adults with Mental Retardation*. Boston, MA: Exceptional Parent Press.

Campling, F. and Sharpe, M. (2006) *Living with a Long-term Illness: The Facts*. Oxford: Oxford University Press.

Hodges, S. (2003) *Counselling Adults with Learning Disabilities*. Basingstoke: Palgrave Macmillan.

Hollins, S., Avis, A. and Cheverton, S. (1989) *Going into Hospital*. London: Books Beyond Words and Royal College of Psychiatrists.

Hopkins, A. and Appleton, R. (1981) *Epilepsy: The Facts*. Oxford: Oxford University Press.

Luchterhand, C. and Murphy, N. (1998) *Helping Adults with Mental Retardation Grieve a Death Loss*. Philadelphia, PA: Accelerated Development.

Sinason, V. (1992) *Mental Handicap and the Human Condition: New Approaches from the Tavistock*. London: Free Association.

USEFUL ORGANIZATIONS

AND RESOURCES

All websites accessed August 2009.

Age Concern
www.ageconcern.org.uk

Alzheimer's Society UK
www.alzheimers.org.uk

American Academy of Audiology
www.audiology.org

American Academy of Developmental Medicine and Dentistry (AADMD)
www.aadmc.org

American Academy of Hospice and palliative Medicine (AAHPM)
www.aahpm.org

American Association of People with Disabilities
www.aapd.com

American Association on Intellectual and Developmental Disabilities (AAIDD)
www.aaidd.org

American Association on Mental Retardation (AAMR)
www.aamr.org

Anxiety Community Forum
www.anxietyhelp.org

Asperger syndrome
www.aspergersyndrome.co.uk

Audiological Society of Australia
www.audiology.asn.au

Australasian Society for the Study of Intellectual Disability (ASSID)
www.assid.org.au

Autism Spectrum Australia (Aspect)
www.aspect.org.au

BEAT
(formerly Eating Disorders Association)
www.b-eat.co.uk

British Academy of Audiology
www.thebsa.org.uk

British Association for Counselling and Psychotherapy
www.bacp.co.uk

British Association of Occupational Therapists and College of Occupational Therapists
www.cot.co.uk

British Institute of Learning Disabilities (BILD)
www.bild.org.uk

British Psychological Society (BPS)
www.bps.org.uk

Canadian Academy of Audiology
www.canadianaudiology.ca

Canadian disability rights legislation
www.disabilityrights.ca

Challenging Behaviour Foundation (CBF)
www.thecbf.org.uk

Department of Health – Learning Disabilities
www.dh.gov.uk

Department of Health – Mental Health
www.dh.gov.uk/mentalhealth

Depression Alliance
www.depressionalliance.org

Down syndrome Association
www.downs-syndrome.org.uk

Elfrida Society
www.elfrida.com

Epilepsy Action (British Epilepsy Association)
www.epilepsy.org.uk

Epilepsy Foundation of America
www.epilepsyfoundation.org

First Steps
(for people with phobias, obsessive compulsive disorder, etc.)
www.first-steps.org

Foundation for People with Learning Disabilities
www.learningdisabilities.org.uk

Intellectual Disability Network (Australia)
www.home.vicnet.au/-dina/

Learning Disabilities Association of Canada
www.ldac-taac.ca

MDF: the Bipolar Organization
(formerly Manic Depression Fellowship)
www.mdf.org.uk

Mencap
www.mencap.org.uk

Mental Health Act Guide
www.hyperguide.co.uk/mha/index.htm/

Mental Health Care
www.mentalhealthcare.org

Mental Health Association
www.mentalhealth.org.au

Mind
www.mind.org.uk

National Autistic Society
www.nas.org.uk

National Institute on Disability and Rehabilitation Research
www.ed.gov

National Phobics Society
www.phobics-society.org.uk

People First
www.peoplefirstltd.com

People First of Canada
www.peoplefirstofcanada.ca

Respond
(information on sexual abuse for people with learning disabilities)
www.respond.org.uk

Royal College of Nursing
www.rcn.org.uk

Royal College of Psychiatry
www.rcpsych.ac.uk

Royal National Institute for Deaf People
www.rnid.org.uk

SANE
www.sane.org.uk

Scope
(for people with cerebral palsy)
www.scope.org.uk

Senior Citizens support in US
www.usa.gov.Topics/Seniors/shtml

Senior Citizens support in Australia
www.seniors.gov.au/internet/seniors/publishing

US disability rights legislation
www.ada.g

INDEX